SUBSTANCE ABUSE PREVENTION ACTIVITIES FOR ELEMENTARY CHILDREN

Timothy A. Gerne, Jr., Ed.D.

Professor, School of Education
The William Paterson College of New Jersey

Patricia J. Gerne, R.N., C.A.C.

Counselor
The Family Program of
Addiction Rehabilitation Treatment Services
(The A.R.T.S.)

Illustrated by Eileen Gerne Ciavarella

Prentice-Hall, Inc.
Englewood Cliffs, New Jersey

Prentice-Hall International, Inc., *London*
Prentice-Hall of Australia Pty. Ltd., *Sydney*
Prentice-Hall Canada Inc., *Toronto*
Prentice-Hall of India Private Ltd., *New Delhi*
Prentice-Hall of Japan, Inc., *Tokyo*
Prentice-Hall of Southeast Asia Pte. Ltd., *Singapore*
Whitehall Books, Ltd., *Wellington, New Zealand*
Editora Prentice-Hall do Brasil Ltda., *Rio de Janeiro*
Prentice-Hall Hispanoamericana, S.A., *Mexico*

TO OUR CHILDREN AND THEIR SPOUSES . . .

. . . Mary and Dennis, Tim and Brandy, Jean,
Eileen and Paul, Kathy, Margaret, Donna,
Danny and Deb, Rosemary, and Michael

AND TO THEIR CHILDREN . . .

. . . Megan, Timothy, Gina, and Chris

Library of Congress Cataloging-in-Publication Data

Gerne, Timothy A.
  Substance abuse prevention activities for elementary children.

  1. School children—United States—Substance use.
2. Substance abuse—United States—Prevention.
3. Activity programs in education—United States.
I. Gerne, Patricia J.   II.   Title.
HV4999.C45G47   1986   372.3'7   86-3176

ISBN 0-13-859075-3

ABOUT THE AUTHORS

TIMOTHY A. GERNE, Ed.D., is a professor in the School of Education's Department of Curriculum and Instruction at The William Paterson College of New Jersey in Wayne. He has worked as an educator of elementary schoolteachers, with a focus in science, for over 30 years. Dr. Gerne is currently Chairperson of the Education Committee to the Local Advisory Committee on Alcoholism for Passaic County, New Jersey.

PATRICIA J. GERNE is a Registered Nurse and a Certified Alcoholism Counselor (C.A.C.) with an extensive background in the field of addiction treatment and prevention. Her involvement during the last 12 years has included using her skills in a long-term in-patient rehabilitation facility, a detoxification unit, and a short-term in-patient rehabilitation unit. Mrs. Gerne is presently a counselor in the Family Program of The A.R.T.S, a comprehensive out-patient addiction treatment program.

DR. AND MRS. GERNE, the parents of ten children, lecture and present workshops in the area of substance abuse prevention for grades K–6 throughout New Jersey.

ABOUT THIS BOOK

Substance Abuse Prevention Activities for Elementary Children was written for teachers and guidance counselors of grades K–6 to use in making children aware of the dangers of substance abuse early enough in life so that growth and development are not hindered. Alcohol and drug abuse can cause pain and devastation for everyone concerned. The longer the drug use continues, interrupting the completion of normal growth and development tasks, the more difficult is the road to recovery.

Prevention requires more than providing information. It includes teaching at the child's developmental level those skills needed for forming a positive self-image, decision-making and coping strategies, and personal values and attitudes, as well as presenting concrete facts. Because most of the material on substance abuse prevention is directed to junior high and high school students, and since many children have already been experimenting with alcohol and drugs at those ages, earlier education is imperative.

Although primary substance abuse prevention begins within the family before elementary school, educators can be an important influence on young children. Therefore, over 50 activities have been prepared for classroom use. Divided by grade levels, these activities are effective, easy to use, and fun. Here is a sampling of what you'll find:

- "Feelings Are Okay" for grades K–1 helps children to identify their own feelings and the feelings of others. This activity encourages the children to develop a positive self-image.

- "Making Choices" for grades 2–3 makes children aware of the need to make choices in solving problems. This activity improves their decision-making abilities.

- "Smoking Is Dangerous to Your Health" for grade 4 focuses on cigarette smoking as the cause of serious health problems. This activity improves children's decision-making and coping skills.

- "Alcohol and Its Effects on the Body's Organs" for grade 5 helps children to identify the physical and behavioral effects of alcohol on the brain and other body organs. This activity clarifies children's attitudes and values.

- "Positive Peer Pressure" for grade 6 helps children become aware of their power to influence others. This activity improves children's self-images.

Each activity includes at least one ready-to-use activity sheet for you to reproduce and distribute to your students. Also provided with each grade level is a letter

iv

you can send to parents to let them know of your substance abuse prevention program.

At the end of the book are five appendices that provide you with more information on substance abuse, as well as the answer keys to the crossword puzzles and word searches.

You do not have to be an "expert" on drugs to use this book. The best opportunity for success is to integrate the ideas and components of the curriculum into daily current activities rather than providing isolated, brief exposure to the topics by "specialists." Teachers and counselors will recognize many of the concepts and objectives contained in this curriculum as basic to the development of the child and the preparation for life in a broad sense. You may modify the activities for other grade levels to meet the needs of your students. The activities have been used successfully in suburban, urban, public, private, and parochial school settings by substance abuse and elementary school counselors as well as by parents.

It is our hope that you will use *Substance Abuse Prevention Activities* to assist young people to arrive at healthy, constructive attitudes about their future use of tobacco, alcohol, and other drugs.

Tim and Pat Gerne

ACKNOWLEDGMENTS

We wish to acknowledge the professional and personal support of our friends and colleagues, especially:

Robert Callahan, Ph.D., Professor of Anatomy and Physiology, The William Paterson College of New Jersey;

Irene Montella, Ph.D., English Department, Ramapo High School, Franklin Lakes, New Jersey;

Margaret Wilczynski, Basic Skills Improvement Teacher (BSIT), Wayne, New Jersey;

Donald Wilczynski, Pharmacist;

Elizabeth Barnet, Registered Nurse, Certified Alcoholism Counselor, Board Member of Local Advisory Committee on Alcoholism of Passaic County, New Jersey;

Lawrence Barnet, M.D., Internist, Board Member of the Impaired Physicians Committee of the Medical Society of New Jersey;

John Manz, former Superintendent of Schools for Franklin Lakes, New Jersey—for allowing activities in this book to be used in that elementary school system during his tenure;

Evelyn Fazio, editor—for her confidence in this project, as well as her support and assistance to us in preparing this manuscript.

We take special delight in thanking our children for their good cheer, comforting support, and real assistance in completing this project. It was a pleasure to collaborate with our daughter, Eileen, who produced the art for this book.

CONTENTS

Contents

–1–

AN OVERVIEW

Drug prevention efforts must focus on *people* and the factors that influence their *behavior*. Teachers' attitudes, children's developmental needs, and the classroom environment will be addressed to provide a basis for understanding the activities presented in chapters three through seven.

Scare tactics and preaching are the least successful approaches in making significant long-term behavioral changes in young people. To have a lasting effect, drug education programs need to present accurate information about alcohol and other drugs, as well as the skills to deal with personal and social growth. There also needs to be an awareness that the student will bring *feelings, attitudes,* and *values* to the learning experience.

Jean Piaget, the Swiss psychologist renowned for his work dealing with how children learn, found that intellectual activity could not be separated from the "total" functioning of the child. Cognitive or intellectual development is only one part of growth and development. Another major aspect is *affective* development, which is concerned with emotions, values, and feelings. All behavior has both affective and intellectual or cognitive aspects. Therefore, *feelings become factors in deciding what to do and what not to do.* (See Figure 1–1—Maslow's Hierarchy of Needs.) The affective domain provides an important link between the *content* learned, and the *behavior* of the child. Affectiveness then, should permeate all that takes place in the classroom. It is both an aid to internalization and an aid to processing information into memory. All experiences are stored for future reference. Positive experiences, which are appropriate for the child's age and competence, build confidence.

Education flourishes in an *environment* rather than a *program.* Alcohol, tobacco, and other drug education is a "process" in that the individual internalizes the processes of self-knowledge, value judgment, decision making, and the assumption of personal responsibility for his or her behavior toward drug use or nonuse. By recognizing this reality, you as the teacher are responsible for creating an atmosphere in which the child can relate to that information *affectively*, from his or her own experiences.

THE TEACHER

It is clear that the elementary schoolteacher is a significant factor in the life of a child. The teacher's role as model, as well as the length of time and the degree of interaction with the student, can have far-reaching effects on the emotional and intellectual development of the child. Since modeling is not a conscious act, the children learn more by example than by being taught, advised, ordered, or directed. Students learn more from what they observe in school, in the home, and from peers than they do in formal classroom instruction. They need to experience people who are worthy role-models.

Since the child's personality is in the formative stage during the primary grades, you, as the elementary schoolteacher, are in a position to exert a powerful positive influence in assisting the student to develop a healthy self-image, and to acquire the skills necessary to deal with his or her world. Stress reduction techniques can be taught to provide immediate and effective tools to handle internal pressures.

FIGURE 1–1

The humanist psychologist Abraham Maslow theorized that basic *needs motivate* human *behavior*. He identified and clarified the interaction between *internal needs* and *external satisfactions*.

MASLOW'S HIERARCHY OF NEEDS

UNMET NEEDS CREATE:

5. Lack of full use of potential.

4. *LACK OF SELF-WORTH*

   Feelings of insecurity and inferiority. Anxiety about personal worth.

3. *UNLOVED–ISOLATED*

   Feelings of loneliness, rejection, and alienation.

2. *LACK OF STABILITY*

   Feelings of fear due to chaos and disorganization.

1. *LACK OF BASIC NEEDS*

   Preoccupation with survival. Physical suffering.

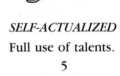

SELF-ACTUALIZED
Full use of talents.
5

SELF-WORTH
Confidence in oneself to master one's world. Need for achievement and competence. Recognition of status from others.
4

BELONGING–LOVE
Risk reaching out for affection, friends, and acceptance.
3

SAFETY
Order, structure, limits. A stable, routine, predictable environment from which to reach out.
2

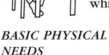

BASIC PHYSICAL NEEDS
Food, shelter, air, and sleep.
1

Drug prevention must focus on *people* and the factors that influence their *behavior*. Feelings become factors in what we do—and what we don't do.

The practice of nonjudgmental interaction by sharing thoughts and feelings in a supportive, accepting environment opens up the possibilities for honest communication and creative exploration. The personal quality of the teacher that enhances a positive relationship with the child is *genuineness*: a caring for the student which is not based on expectations, but is based on respect for the child.

The *attitude* a teacher conveys makes a deeper, more profound impression on the student than all the factual information in a text. Children work better when they feel their teacher cares about them, and where there is substantial use of praise and approval in the classroom setting. It is part of the information from his environment that the child will internalize to create his self-image. One's self-esteem is influenced by the manner in which one is treated. Carl Rogers and other humanistic psychologists believe that the most important aspect of personality evaluation is how the person sees himself. The implications for teachers are clear. Assisting a child to increase his feelings of self-worth will increase his courage to tackle new challenges, as well as encourage him to make constructive decisions about his future. *Self-concept and achievement are positively related.* Students behave better and achieve more when teachers treat them in ways which emphasize their successes and potential for good, rather than those which focus on their failings and shortcomings.

THE CHILD

During the elementary school years, the child is expected to acquire the foundations of learning that are considered essential for successful adjustment to later life. Failure to master the tasks assigned during this period result in feelings of inferiority and insecurity. Success in handling responsibilities will add to a sense of well-being. Elementary schoolchildren, ages six to twelve, are usually thought of as being in middle childhood. Motor abilities improve and the skills to manipulate equipment and materials increase. Children learn by doing—by acting out, by handling objects, by seeing pictures, by hearing stories. Therefore, information must be presented in a concrete form in order for them to absorb it, process it, and assimilate it. Cognitive abilities are expanding and reasoning becomes possible. The activities in this book have been prepared to promote the child's personal growth and development, and to diminish the probability of the use of drugs as a means of meeting their needs.

Grades K–3

The students' primary developmental task is learning to deal with others socially and cooperatively. Concerns of the students embrace the areas of feelings about one's self, one's skills, and one's ability to get along with others. Socializing with peer groups in school and in play is very important. Play groups are formed in which members are usually of the same age, sex, and grade level. This special set of peers participates in most socializing activities together. In this expanded environment, the children will begin to modify their self-images which had been originally established by interacting primarily with family. During this four-year span, the children will learn that what they do affects others and is of concern to others. During this period the children are strongly influenced by adults. The teacher can build on the students' burgeoning acceptance of themselves as persons in their own right, with unique talents and worthwhile skills.

As part of the individual maturation process, the children will, of course, experience negative feelings. Children should learn constructive alternatives to handling anger, fear, frustration, anxiety, loneliness, and jealousy. Teachers should discuss healthy ways to handle stress and upset feelings through exercise, relaxation, play, and talking with others. The children can begin to understand that problem solving and decision making are dynamic processes. By practicing problem-solving skills, they will know that more than one choice is available; that each choice has its advantages and disadvantages in terms of positive and negative consequences when they make a decision. The negative concepts of running away, denying that problems exist, or avoiding problems should be discussed. Authority figures such as parents, teachers, and police officers should be presented as potential "helping" people. The teacher can help the students to understand and develop a respect for rules and the law.

In these grades, emphasis should also be on maintaining good health. Since the children's social encounters are usually narrow at this point, use of drugs, medicines, or experiences with other chemicals will usually occur close to home. Children should be taught respect for medicines and other potentially dangerous substances. They need to know about common medicines and how they are used. For instance, they need to be given the information that drugs used under a doctor's prescription for a definite illness are proper and beneficial. The concepts must be developed that unknown substances might produce harmful physiological or psychological effects. These unknown substances include other people's medicines or pills, substances offered by friends, or those left carelessly within their reach. Children should learn from whom they may accept medicines. Early training to introduce these good health practices should produce proper future attitudes.

Grades 4–6

Concepts presented in earlier grades about mental health and life-coping processes should be further developed. These concepts include how emotions affect behavior, the interaction between feelings and thought processes, the relationship between emotions and body condition, and the effects of self-image in their reactions to criticism or praise. Students can be encouraged to give themselves positive messages and practice healthy alternatives to change negative emotions. The topics of problem solving, decision making, understanding behavior, expressing feelings honestly and constructively, and group belonging and acceptance will be explored. Risk taking, consequences, and alternatives will be addressed.

Other sources of information from peers, television, and older siblings begin to challenge parents as the sole authority. Children, therefore, will need to learn necessary skills to clarify their own value judgments.

Students at this developmental level are becoming aware of their increased responsibility for their own behavior and for the decisions governing the personal alcohol/drug use that they will make in the near future. The potential hazards of alcohol, tobacco, and other drugs to body systems and overall health should be presented. Children need to be informed of the concepts of drug/alcohol use, misuse, and abuse.

THE COMMUNITY

Our children live in a world barraged by information and cues about drugs. There is a constant stream of messages promising magical cures and instantaneous relief. Chemicals appear to be an acceptable way to handle life's problems. *Access* and *acceptance* are key words in explaining a problem of such magnitude in contemporary society.

Families, schools, and communities must join together in a major cooperative effort. Prevention efforts need to include parents, teachers, clergymen, community leaders, and police officers all giving consistent messages:

1. Intoxication by any substance is not acceptable.
2. There are people who care and who are available to offer help and direction.
3. You are each capable of learning *constructive ways* to meet your needs.
4. You can learn and practice these skills.

–2–

STRESS
AND HOW TO REDUCE
ITS EFFECTS

This chapter includes a description of stress, and easily taught, convenient techniques for reducing its effects.

This information is placed in a separate chapter for easy access and use for *all* grade levels. The four main areas covered in this chapter are:

1. Relaxation
2. Exercise
3. Recreation
4. Expressing Feelings

Stress is the physical, mental, and chemical reaction to circumstances that cause fear, excitement, irritation, or endangerment. The mind and the body are inseparable. Mental states and attitudes affect our bodies with a variety of chemical changes, which, in turn, produce other dramatic physical and mental changes.

Buildup of emotions

Expectations and pressures

Low self-esteem. Feelings of power-lessness and inadequacy

Some immediate changes in our body which may be apparent to us when we experience stress are:

Heart palpitations	Tight muscles
Stomachaches	Cold hands
Rapid breathing	Dry mouth
Excess sweating	Dilated pupils

For primitive people, survival depended upon an immediate physiological reaction that prepared them for "fight" or "flight" when they felt threatened. In modern times, we may not immediately discharge this *energy* created to meet the stressors we experience due to social expectations or lack of skills and techniques with which to release the tension.

Allowing these negative physical and emotional tensions to remain unaddressed leads to physical and emotional "dis-ease." Alcohol, tobacco, and other drugs might be used to assist an individual to attain some level of comfort during times of stress. This response can begin an unhealthy pattern of *coping behavior*. Healthy, creative alternatives must be learned. Following are readily available and easily taught "de-stress" skills and techniques that relieve tension, improve self-image, and provide personal satisfaction. The essential element in the success of the alternatives approach is the importance of choosing activities that meet the individual's particular needs and interests.

RELAXATION

Quick Calming Response

1. Recognize some of the body's signals of tension and upset feelings.

2. Turn inward to "see" your happy face, or "listen" inwardly to a word or sound that had been chosen to be used in stressful situations.

3. Slowly take a deep breath, and slowly let it out. Sense the "tense air" going out, and the "calm air" coming in. Repeat the breathing three times.

   It requires no silence or solitude. It requires only several seconds to calm your body.

Relaxation Response

1. In a comfortable chair, in a quiet environment, with the eyes closed:

   a. Concentrate on the breath going in and out. One may choose instead to concentrate on a particular word or sound instead of the breathing.

   b. When the mind begins to wander, gently draw it back to the breath or the word and continue the process.

   Children: 5 to 10 minutes; adults: 15 to 20 minutes

Progressive Relaxation

1. Have the children stiffen all the joints in their extremities to become aware of the general feelings of tension in their bodies. They can parade around the room like wooden soldiers to demonstrate the idea.

2. At the teacher's direction, the students will tense and then relax each muscle group of the body.

3. Through the systematic tensing and relaxing of major isolated muscle groups throughout the body, the individual learns to recognize and to control the "power on" feeling noted under stress and the "power off" feeling of being relaxed.

4. The student can now choose to participate in the progressive relaxation technique alone.

   a. Sit in a comfortable position, in a quiet atmosphere, with the eyes closed.

   b. Begin to relax each muscle group, beginning at the toes and working towards the forehead.

   c. Remain in the totally relaxed position for 5 to 10 minutes.

   d. When ready, slowly open the eyes, and return to normal activities.

Visualization

1. Sit in a quiet place, in a comfortable position with the eyes closed. Begin to relax.

2. Now take a "mini-vacation." Visualize yourself in a scene that gives a feeling of happiness and pleasure. It may be the beach, a mountain scene, a day at a park. Try to be very specific about the scene: how the weather feels; how you are dressed for the occasion, and so forth. Stay there for 10 to 20 minutes.

3. When you choose, open your eyes slowly. Sit quietly for a minute and then resume the day's activities.

When you have done any of these simple relaxation exercises, the feelings of tension should be reduced, your "batteries are recharged," so to speak, and a sense of well-being is evident.

The more regularly these exercises are practiced, the greater is the benefit derived.

POSITIVE RESPONSES

Positive Statements

1. Make a game of replacing negative statements with positive statements about oneself or about a situation.

2. Collect and have readily available a list of positive statements about oneself.

Positive Imagery

1. The body really cannot tell whether an image the mind holds is real or a fantasy. If the image is clearly defined, the body will respond according to the image.

2. Positive images add to feelings of self-mastery and afford a sense of control in one's life.

Good performance   Positive picture power   Winning style

EXERCISE

Physical exercise is an excellent way to rid the body of the effects of stress. Exercise dissipates the effects of stress and helps the body return to normal. It lessens anxiety and depression, and affords a sense of calm and well-being.

stretching

swimming

bending

climbing
aerobics

lifting

jumping rope

jogging

RECREATION

Everyone should arrange a daily time to play. It should be considered a natural good-health practice. It provides diversion for the mind and lets it change its focus from problems to a chosen, personally satisfying, activity.

Many investigators have found that play, particularly play involving make-believe, increases the number of solutions to problems that young children can create. This avenue of fantasy gives them practice in making associations and interpreting imagery.

skate boarding

ice skating

playing ball

enjoying nature

listening to music

play dolls   board games
watch TV   marbles
go to a movie   puzzles
ceramics   painting
row boating   coloring
baseball   sewing

EXPRESS FEELINGS

Probably the most significant way to release tension is to talk one's feelings over with someone else. A very *direct statement* of one's feelings can be most helpful. The other person hears them and acknowledges them. Sometimes that is all that is needed. Drawing pictures of the feelings or keeping a journal or diary can also be helpful.

Express feelings

Talk to a friend

Build intimacy

Develop a support system

–3–
ACTIVITIES FOR GRADES K–1

A. Parent Letter

B. *Activity Titles*

		Objectives
3–1	I Am Special	To become more aware of one's own uniqueness.
3–2	Feelings Are Okay	To identify one's feelings and the feelings of others.
3–3	Coping with Negative Feelings	To identify upset feelings. To explore healthy ways of coping with unhappy and uncomfortable feelings.
3–4	Kindness Is Contagious	To identify and demonstrate ways of reaching out to others.
3–5	Help!	To identify and explore ways of seeking help from others when dealing with problems.
3–6	*Think* Before Acting	To identify feelings when experimenting with new activities. To examine consequences of one's actions.
3–7	Setting Limits	To explore the consequences of excesses.
3–8	Being Responsible	To recognize the importance of accepting responsibility for one's actions.
3–9	Healthy Habits	To learn to make wise choices to maintain good health.
3–10	Safe and Unsafe Substances to Put in My Mouth	To identify and evaluate safe and unsafe substances.
3–11	Coping with Stress	To explore some healthy ways to cope with stressful situations.

Dear Parent,

Activities for kindergarten and first grade students have been prepared, based on sound principles of growth and development, to positively influence your child in forming healthy ways to deal with one's self and others. Addressing these issues *prior* to the time when alcohol and other drug use is most likely to occur increases the probability that your child will not yield to those pressures that frequently lead to substance abuse. These activities will help your child to

1. Become more aware of one's own uniqueness.
2. Identify one's own feelings and the feelings of others.
3. Identify upset feelings and explore healthy ways of coping with unhappy or uncomfortable feelings.
4. Identify and demonstrate ways of reaching out to others.
5. Identify and explore ways of seeking help from others when dealing with problems.
6. Identify feelings when experimenting with new activities and examine the consequences of one's actions.
7. Explore the consequences of excesses.
8. Recognize the importance of accepting responsibility for his or her actions.
9. Learn to make wise choices to maintain good health and identify and evaluate safe and unsafe substances to put into one's mouth.
10. Explore some healthy ways to cope with stressful situations.

We cannot protect our children from facing many of the problems of growing up in today's society, but we can prepare them for this task. Your interest, support, and caring interaction will assist your child in arriving at healthy attitudes and skills.

_____
Teacher

3–1

I AM SPECIAL

Objective

To help the children become more aware of their own uniqueness.

Purpose

To develop a positive self-image.
To clarify personal attitudes and values.

Activities

Explore ways in which the children can recognize that they are "special."

1. Create an "Award Picture." See the "Award Picture" activity sheet (3–1A).

   a. Ask the children to bring in a personal photo. Paste it in the center of the frame as shown in the illustration. Draw lines from the four corners of the frame inward, to the tip of the photo, creating a mat border. Color the frame and matting each a different color. Cut them out. Color the award ribbon. Cut it out. Paste it on the picture.

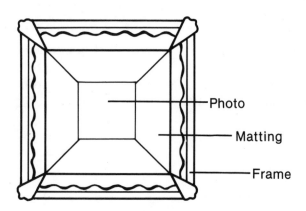

   b. The project may be pasted onto a piece of cardboard of the same size to add support.

   c. It may be hung up in the classroom or in a prominent place in the home.

   d. Talk about the fact that each person is unique and special.

2. Discuss how "special" it is to be a boy or a girl. Complete the "I'm Lucky to Be Me" activity sheet (3–1B).

    a. Instruct the children to trace the letters of the word that is "right" for them.

    b. Add facial features.

    c. Color the hair and eyes, using their own hair and eye colors.

3. Tell a happy story they remember, or have heard someone in their family tell about them, when they were a baby or small child.

4. Have the children celebrate their own "special" birthday, as shown in the "Come to My Party" activity sheet (3–1C).

    a. Color the cake.

    b. Select the appropriate age candle. Color it and cut it out. Place it on the birthday cake.

    c. Draw three friends into the picture whom they might invite to the celebration.

    d. Talk about how it feels to have one's own special party or celebration each year.

5. Learn the holidays which are important in the children's homes. Discuss how the holidays are celebrated. Have the students create decorations used during one of the celebrations and share their significance with the class.

6. Each morning for a week ask the children to look in the mirror before coming to school and say, "Good morning, _____." Ask each child to say
                                        the child's name

one positive thing about him- or herself into the mirror.

To assist the children in choosing a sentence to use, you can offer several "Positive Stroke" sentences:

Positive Strokes for Being	*Positive Strokes for Doing*
I am a pleasure.	I like the way I _____.
I'm glad you are here.	I am really improving.
Good morning _____ (name).	I'm proud of the way I _____.
I'm glad to share this day.	I can _____ very well.
I am unique.	
I am important.	
I like me.	
I'm glad I was born.	

> *Note: The teacher or parent may read the directions in the Activity Pages to the children.*

Reminder:

I AM UNIQUE

Name _____

Date _____

Award Picture

Color ribbon.
Cut out ribbon.
Paste on the side of
the frame.

I'm Lucky to Be Me

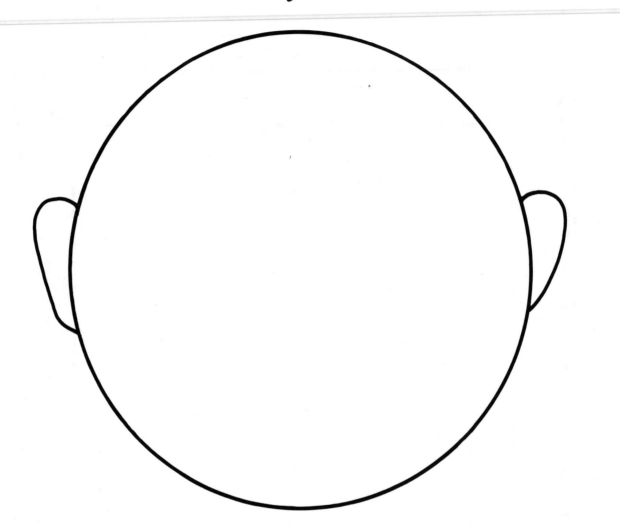

I AM LUCKY TO BE A _____ paste the word here _____ .

1. Trace the words

2. Cut out the word that is right for you.

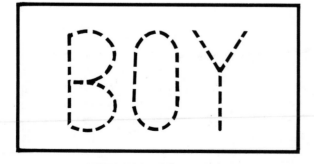

Come to My Party

Color and cut out your age candle.

3–2

FEELINGS ARE OKAY

Objective

To have children identify their own feelings and the feelings of others. The children will practice different ways of expressing feelings.

Purpose

To develop a positive self-image.
To clarify personal values and attitudes.

Activities

> *Note: Tell the students that feelings are neither right nor wrong. You are responsible for your own behavior.*

1. Demonstrate different ways people express their feelings using the four "feeling" face cards as shown in the "Feeling Faces" activity sheet (3–2A). Cut out the pictures along the dotted line and paste them on cardboard. Give one of the children a feeling card without showing it to the group. The child acts out the emotion on the card. The class must guess the feeling.

2. Instruct the children to cut out the eyebrows and mouth from the "Making Faces" activity sheet (3–2B). They may arrange them on the picture to create different expressions. Invite a child to tell a story in which he or she would "feel" that way.

3. Cut out pictures of people from magazines and newspapers. Have the children tell what emotions they think are visible in each picture.

4. Play different pieces of music. Have the children act out an emotion they *feel* when they listen to it. (All feelings will be accepted.)

5. Have the children complete open-ended sentences. Reproduce the feeling faces for each child. Cut out along the dotted line. Each child may hold up one of the feeling cards to answer.

    Examples:

    When I see people fighting I feel _____.

    I feel _____ when the teacher smiles at me.

    When someone hurts my feelings I feel _____.

I feel _____ when someone says something unkind to me.

I feel _____ when my friend doesn't play with me.

I feel _____ when I have to go to school.

6. Discuss acceptable and unacceptable ways of showing our feelings. The teacher may read the sentences aloud. The children may raise their hands when they identify a feeling. They may clap once if they identify a behavior.

Examples: (Feelings will be underlined. Behaviors will be circled to identify them here.)

a. Is it okay to be <u>angry</u>?

b. Should you (make believe) you are not <u>angry</u> or <u>hurt</u> when you are?

c. May boys (cry) when they are <u>hurt</u>?

d. Is it okay to (hit) someone when you are <u>angry</u>?

e. Should I (tell someone) when I feel <u>sad</u>?

f. Can I (ask for help) when I am <u>scared</u>?

g. Is it okay to '(punch a pillow)' when I feel <u>angry</u>?

Reminder:

FEELINGS ARE OKAY

Feeling Faces

MAD

GLAD

SAD

SCARED

''FEELING CARDS''—Cut out along dotted lines.

Making Faces

eyebrows

mouths

Cut out eyebrows and mouths and create different expressions on this face. Talk about each one.

3–3

COPING WITH NEGATIVE FEELINGS

Objective

To teach the children to identify upset feelings and begin to explore healthy ways of coping with unhappy and uncomfortable feelings.

Purpose

To improve coping skills.
To clarify personal values and attitudes.

Activities

Note: Give the children "permission" to accept and talk about uncomfortable feelings. Acknowledge that everyone has uncomfortable and unhappy feelings sometimes.

---

1. Have the children cut out pictures in a magazine or newspaper showing people who look upset. Have the children tell a story about each one.

2. Have the children describe some body sensations that they may experience when they feel scared, sad, or mad. For example, you may ask the students:

   "Do you ever get "butterflies" in your stomach before you try something new?"

   "Do you get "sweaty" hands when you are scared?"

   "Do you get jittery, because you feel like running away when you are scared?"

   "Do you sometimes feel very tired when you are sad?"

   You may share some of your personal experiences also.

3. Have a child role-play being lost. How would he or she feel? Ask: What would you do? Why? Have the class offer suggestions to find a solution.

4. Have a child role-play interacting with a friend who has broken his toy. What would the child do? Have the class give suggestions.

5. Have two children role-play with paper dolls or finger puppets.

   a. One child expresses an emotion. The other child responds with his or her feeling by acting it out.

Example: One child appears to be (crying) because he has hurt himself. The other child may decide to (console) him or (scold) him, as he chooses.

Explore advantages and disadvantages of each behavior.

6. Have the children complete the unfinished sentences, focusing on behaviors:

When I am <u>angry</u> I _____.

When I am <u>tired</u> I _____.

When I am <u>hurt</u> I _____.

When no one wants to play with me I _____.

Reminder:

FEELINGS ARE OKAY

3–4

KINDNESS IS CONTAGIOUS

Objective

To have the children identify and demonstrate ways of reaching out to others.

Purpose

To improve decision making.
To improve communication.
To clarify personal values.
To develop social responsibility.

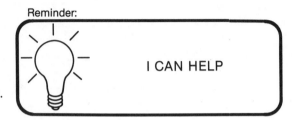

Activities

> *Note: You can give instructions for this activity at the beginning of the day. Instructions can continue throughout a normal schoolday.*

1. Cut out the flowers from the ''Planting the Seed'' activity sheet (3–4A). Color the flowers. Give a flower to a child. Have a child perform an act of kindness for another student. Let the first child then give the flower to that student who will then perform an act of kindness for another student when a need is noticed, thus passing the flower along to him or her, and so on.

   Examples: Picking up a dropped pencil, sharing something, holding a door open, and so forth.

2. Have the children discuss the feelings they get when they are kind to others. Ask them: How do you feel when someone is kind to you?

3. Discuss how acts of kindness proliferate and affect others around them.

4. Have the children take home the cut-out flowers and perform an act of kindness for someone there. Ask them to explain the exercise to their families.

5. Play games in which the responsibility for success is shared. Discuss how it feels being part of an activity.

6. Learn a song about helping.

7. Cut out the helping hand from the ''Helping Hand'' activity sheet (3–4B). When the children give someone in the class a ''helping hand,'' they may pass it on to another student. Each person who participates over the course of the day may add their names on the helping hand. Talk about how ''contagious'' or ''catching'' kindness is. The children may also trace the outlines of their own hands, and use it as the ''helping hand.''

Name _____

Date _____

Planting the Seed

1. Color the flowers and cut them out.
2. Help someone and plant the "seeds of kindness."

Name _____

Date _____

Helping Hand

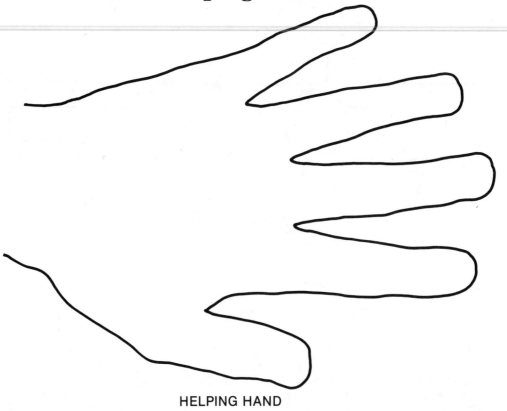

HELPING HAND

You may trace your hand here.

3–5

HELP!

Objective

To have the children identify and explore ways of seeking help from others when dealing with their problems.

Purpose

To improve decision-making skills.
To add coping skills.
To improve communication.

Activities

Note: Stress the fact that everyone *at some time needs help.*

---

1. Discuss situations at home in which the children might need help. Role-play the situation. Explore the feelings involved and some solutions to the problem.

   Examples: What would you do if. . . .

   a. A cup is out of reach on a high shelf.

   b. Your ball rolls into the busy street.

   c. Your little brother falls and hurts himself.

   d. You're not sure of what is in a certain container that someone else tells you contains soda.

2. Discuss situations at school in which the children might need help. Role-play. How would you feel in these situations? Ask: What would you do to get help if:

   a. You become ill and there is no one around to help.

   b. You forgot to bring your lunch to school.

   c. An older child in an upper grade is bullying you.

3. Create paper-cup puppets suggested in the "Who Will Help?" activity sheet (3–5A). Role-play:

   a. nurse—patient

   b. dentist—child

   c. mother—hurt child

   d. school friend—lonely child

   Do you ask for help when you need it? What happens?

4. Have the children cut out pictures in magazines and newspapers that show people helping others. Discuss the pictures selected.

   Examples: a. An ambulance at the scene of an accident

   b. A police officer helping someone

5. Have each of the children draw a picture of three loving, caring people they know, using the "People Who Care About Me" activity sheet (3–5B). When the assignment has been completed, the teacher will lead a discussion. Ask the students:

   Who are they?

   How do they show they are loving, caring people (hugging, listening, helping, etc.)?

   Do you ask them for help when you need it?

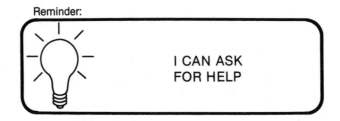

Name _____

Date _____

Who Will Help?

Use

1. paper cups
2. marker or crayons

Directions

1. Turn the paper cups upside down.
2. Make faces with marker or a crayon.
3. Insert your hand into the cup to move the puppet.

_____Add a bow for a girl.

_____Add a cap for a boy.

To create headpieces to identify helpers:

Use: oaktag or construction paper, marker or crayons, a pair of scissors, glue or staples.

Directions: After creating headpiece, cut out and attach the headpiece to the top of the paper cups.

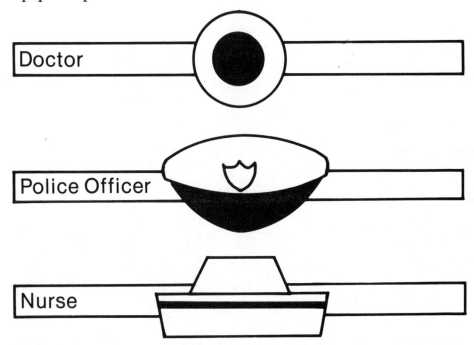

Doctor

Police Officer

Nurse

Make more headpieces to identify helpers.

People Who Care About Me

_____

_____

_____

Draw a picture of three loving, caring people you know.

3–6

THINK BEFORE ACTING

Objective

To have children identify their feelings when experimenting with new activities and examine the consequences of their actions.

Purpose

To clarify personal values.
To improve decision-making skills.

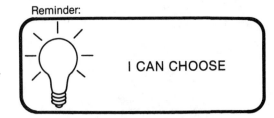

Reminder:

I CAN CHOOSE

Activities

1. Discuss with the children feelings they may have before beginning to do something new.

2. Blindfold a child. Hand him or her objects of different consistencies without telling what they are. Discuss the feelings involved with dealing with the unknown.

3. The children may role-play people in new situations such as these:

   a. A new school term

   b. A new teacher

   c. A first airplane ride

4. Ask the students:

   a. If you thought of what might happen before you try something new, would it make a difference in whether or not you would do it?

   b. If your friend fell off his bike while trying to "pop a wheelie" or ride down a steep driveway, would you try it anyway? If he said it was fun, would you do it even after he got hurt? Why?

   c. If you didn't want to do it because you were afraid, and someone called you a "baby," would you try it then? Why?

5. Follow the maze on the "Choosing the Safe Path" activity sheet (3–6A) to arrive safely at the park. Talk about unsafe things in the picture. Tell them to *choose the safe path*.

6. Discuss how thinking about the consequences first might influence our actions. What may happen if

   a. You cross the street on a red light?

   b. Your teacher gives you a homework assignment, but instead of doing it you go out to play?

   c. You go to your friend's house after school without telling one of your parents?

Teach the children that they can choose the safe ways of doing things.

Name _____

Date _____

Choosing the Safe Path

Choose
the right path.

3–7

SETTING LIMITS

Objective

To explore some of the consequences of excesses.

Purpose

To improve decision-making skills.
To develop coping skills.

Activities

> *Note: Stress the fact that everyone has limits.*

1. Ask three different sized children of apparently different strengths to hold out their arms. Begin to pile books onto their arms until each must drop the load. Can they all hold the same number of books? When is it too much? Should you tell someone when you get uncomfortable—*before* it is too much?

2. Play a radio at a pleasant sound level. Inquire about the children's level of comfort. Increase the sound volume. Discuss how they feel now. Is it too much for some students and comfortable for others? What should they do about it?

3. Complete the "The Girl Who Had Too Much Soda" activity sheet (3–7A). Ask the students how they might feel in the same situation. How could it have been prevented? Would they do it differently the next time?

4. Ask the children, how do you feel when:

   a. You stay up late and are very tired?

   b. You have too much cake and candy at a birthday party?

   c. You stay in the sun too long?

   d. You play too hard on a very hot day?

5. Take two different sized containers and fill each one to the top with water or sand. Pour the water out of the smaller one. Pour the contents of the larger container into the smaller container. Is there too much for *that particular* container? Help the students recognize that each container was full and useful, but *different* with its own *unique limits*.

Reminder: I AM UNIQUE

Name _____

Date _____

The Girl Who Had Too Much Soda

Gina had _6_ cans of soda. How many more cans of soda make _6_? Cut out or circle the correct number below.

3–8

BEING RESPONSIBLE

Objective

To have the children recognize the importance of accepting responsibility for their actions.

Purpose

To develop coping skills.
To clarify personal values.
To develop social responsibility.

Activities

1. Have the teacher define the word *responsibility*. Ask for responses from the children to clarify their understanding of what it means.

2. Explore several ways of helping other people, such as: grandparents, classmates, the teacher, or a younger child.

3. Determine what responsibilities each child may have at home. Some examples would be: hanging up your clothes, walking the dog, cleaning your room, caring for a younger brother or sister.

4. Have a child role-play a responsibility that he or she has in the home. See if the class can guess what it is.

5. Discuss the responsibilities of different people in the community such as: school custodian, clergy, doctor, teacher, garbage collector, and mailcarrier. What might happen if they neglected their responsibilities? The children may create finger puppets or paper-cup puppets to role-play this activity.

6. The children can see the need to accept responsibility when they see the results of neglect. Try this activity. Have the children plant flower seeds in several different containers. Discuss the fact that plants need air, light, and water. Assign several students to be responsible for giving selected plants proper care. Keep a record of the results. Indicate on other seed containers that they will *not* be given one or all of the things they need for growth. What happens to these plants?

7. Have the students complete the "Spreading Sunshine" activity sheet (3–8A). The child may write or draw something he or she has done during the day to be responsible in the cloud. Have the child write his or her name in the sun. Add extra "sunshine" by coloring the picture. Follow the numbers for colors:

1—yellow

2—orange

3—red

8. Have the children explore the difference between accidental and deliberate acts that hurt others. Ask: How do you feel when you have been hurt?
How do you think someone else may feel?
What can we do to make others feel good again after they have been hurt?

Reminder:

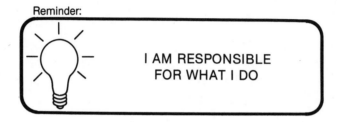

I AM RESPONSIBLE
FOR WHAT I DO

Name _____

Date _____

Spreading Sunshine

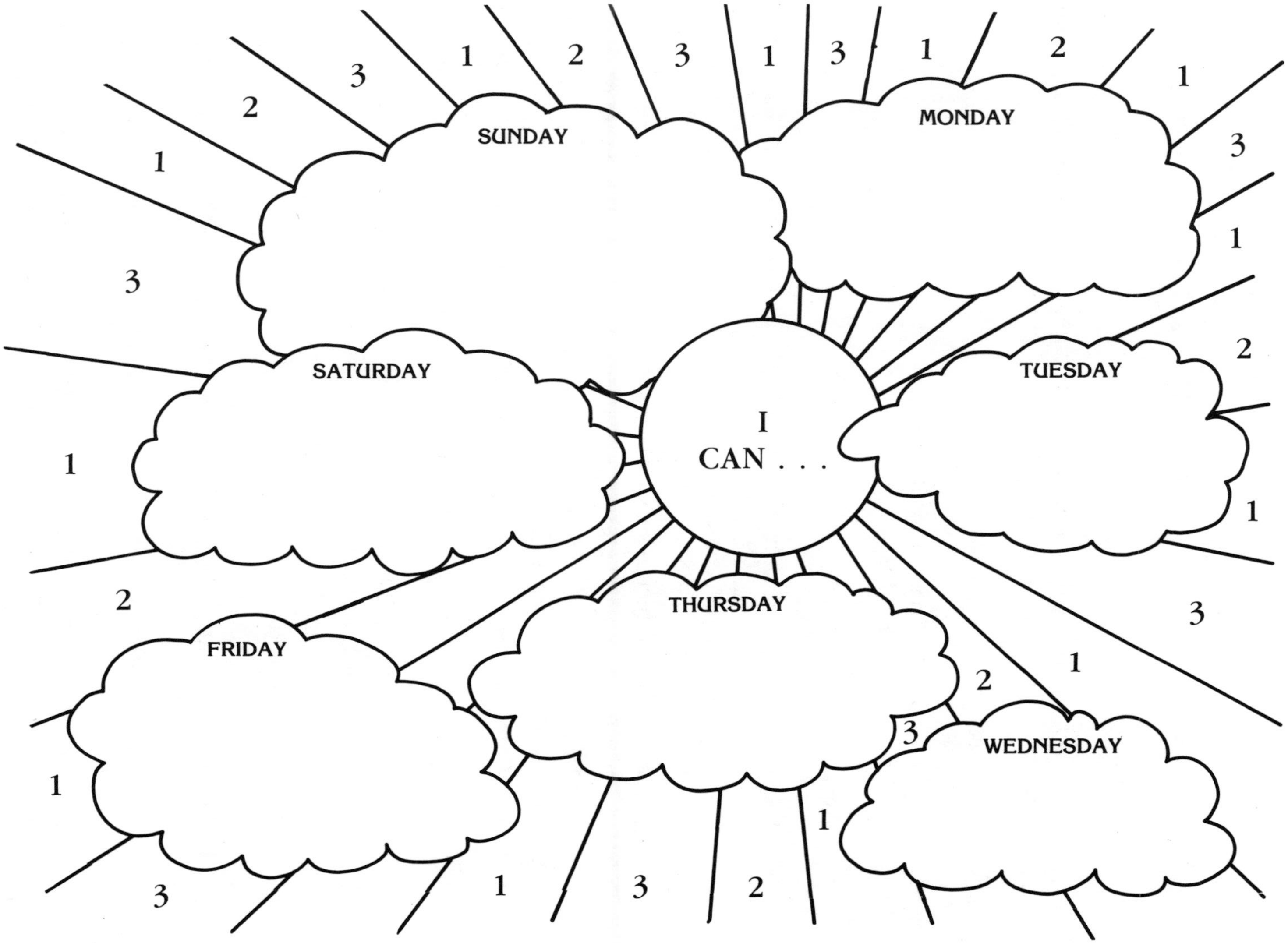

Color the numbered areas:

1 = yellow
2 = orange
3 = red

I CAN . . . .

MONDAY

TUESDAY

WEDNESDAY

THURSDAY

FRIDAY

SATURDAY

SUNDAY

3–9

HEALTHY HABITS

Objective

To teach the children to make wise choices to maintain their personal good health.

Purpose

To improve decision-making skills.
To develop good health practices.

Activities

1. Discuss some good daily hygiene habits that must be done each day, using "I _____."

2. Have each child complete the activities in the "Healthy Habits Matching Game" activity sheet (3–9A).

   a. Match the pictures to show good health habits.

   b. Discuss what would happen if one did not do these things each day.

3. Discuss the need to dress appropriately for the weather. "I _____." Explore what would happen if we did not do this.

4. Complete the exercise shown in the "Rose" activity sheet (3–9B) by:

   a. coloring the doll and giving it a name

   b. cutting out the paper doll

5. Complete the "Keeping Warm" activity sheet (3–9C) by:

   a. coloring Rose's clothes

   b. cutting out the warm clothes

   c. dressing Rose

   d. making more clothes

6. Have the children cut out pictures of clothing for all types of weather from magazines.

7. Talk about games that can be played in different types of weather, such as indoor and outdoor games.

8. Talk about the need for a good night's sleep. Ask the children: What would happen if you did not get enough sleep for a few days? Ask them to share personal experiences.

9. Have the children complete the "Setting the Clock" activity sheet (3–9D). Have them:

   a. Cut along the lines in the eye slots.

   b. Cut out the hands on the page and attach them to the clock with a fastener.

   c. Cut out the eye strips. The strips should be inserted in the eye slots. The eyes may be moved to reinforce sleeping and waking time. The hands may be moved from bedtime to wakeup time.

10. Discuss with the children why it is important to get a checkup from the doctor. Talk about the physician as a helper.

Reminder:

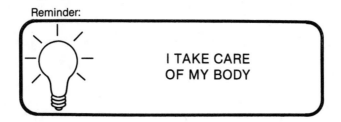

I TAKE CARE
OF MY BODY

Healthy Habits
Matching Game

Draw a line to the opposite side to help the child stay healthy.

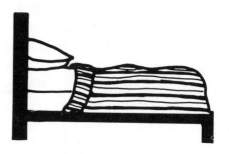

Rose

Cut out the paper doll.

Name _____

Date _____

Keeping Warm

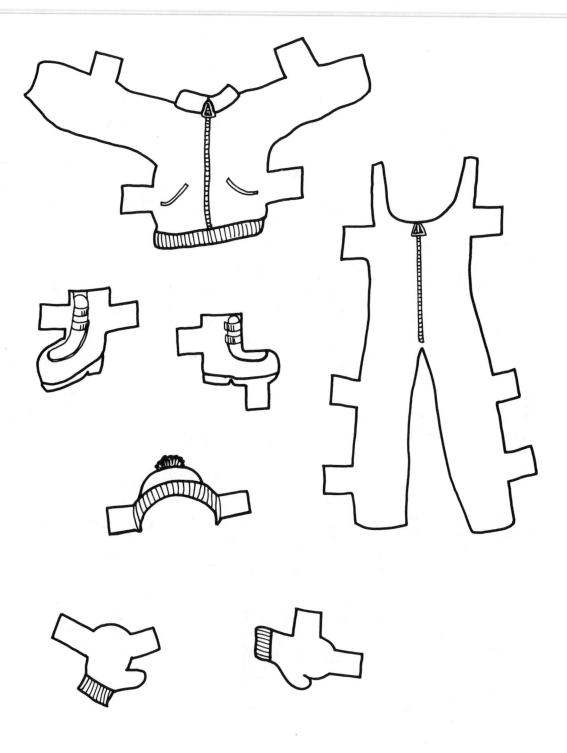

Dress the paper doll with warm winter clothes. Cut out her clothes.

Name _____

Date _____

Setting the Clock

Cut along dotted lines of eye slots.

Cut out "hands" for the clock.

Cut along dotted line.

EYE STRIPS

Insert eye strips in eye slots on the clock.

3–10

SAFE AND UNSAFE SUBSTANCES
TO PUT IN MY MOUTH

Objective

To teach the children to identify and evaluate healthy and unhealthy substances to put into their mouths.

Purpose

To improve decision-making skills.
To develop good health practices.
To demonstrate personal care as a sign of their worth.

Activities

1. Discuss the need to eat the proper foods to maintain strength and health, including the four food groups. Ask the children to

   a. Cut out the pictures of foods from newspapers and magazines that are good for us.

   b. Draw a picture of their favorite food.

   c. Ask what food do you not like at all? You may help the student find something else to eat that has the same food value.

   d. Discuss overeating as harmful to the body. (Refer back to the ''The Girl Who Had Too Much Soda'' (3–7A) activity sheet.)

2. Discuss the importance of not putting unknown substances into your mouth.

   a. The teacher may develop the shoe box activity described on the next page to identify which substances are safe and which are unsafe to put into one's mouth.

   b. Have the children complete the ''What's Good for Me'' activity sheet (3–10A) by putting an X over those things that are unhealthy for children. Draw a line from the article to the body to indicate those items that are acceptable for children.

Reminder:

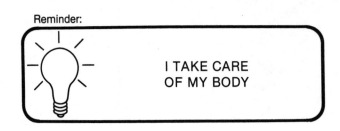

I TAKE CARE
OF MY BODY

Use

1. two shoe boxes
2. a pair of scissors to cut an opening in the top of the boxes
3. materials to decorate

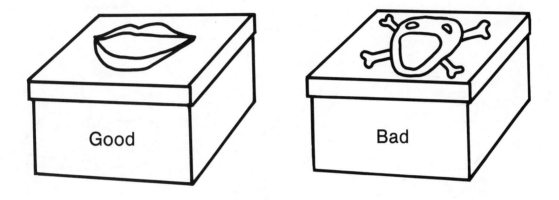

Directions

1. Cut out an opening in the top of each box. Decorate to reinforce the idea of the exercise.

2. Have the children cut out pictures of items from old magazines and newspapers that are safe to put into their mouths, and things that are unsafe to put into their mouths. Place them in the proper boxes.

3. When the boxes are filled, the contents may be emptied and reviewed to support good health practices.

Name _____

Date _____

What's Good for Me

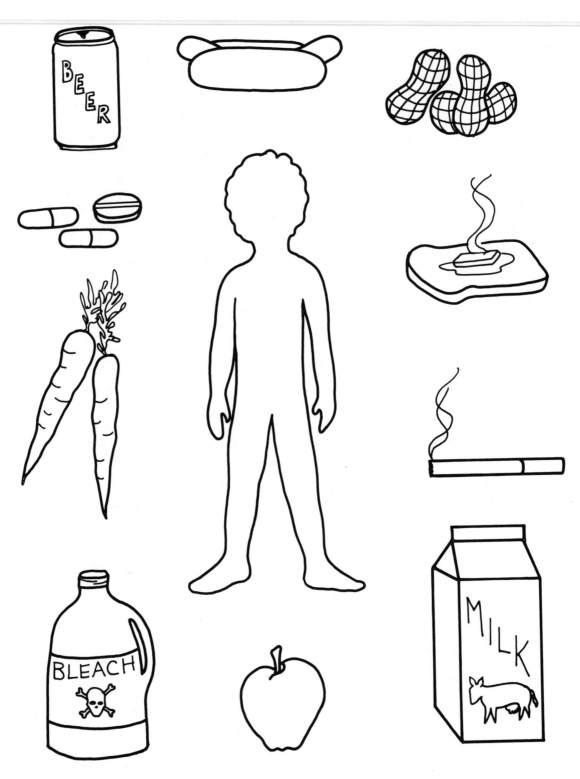

Cross out unsafe things to put in your mouth.
Draw a line to the body for safe things to put in your mouth.

3–11

COPING WITH STRESS

Objective

To make the childen become aware of healthy ways to cope with stressful situations.

Purpose

To increase coping skills by learning natural ways of relaxing and handling uncomfortable feelings.

Activities

> *Note: Discuss with the children some of the things they might feel in their bodies when they have bad or upset feelings.* Examples: *tight muscles, headache, perspiration, shaky knees, stomachache, etc.*

Direct the children in the following exercises:

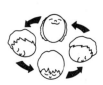

1. *Head Roll* to relax the neck muscles and increase circulation. Tell children: Close your eyes; sit up straight in your chair; roll the head slowly in a complete circle first one way and then the other.

2. *Rag Doll* to relax and increase circulation. Instruct students: Stand next to your seat. Close your eyes. Slowly bend forward at the waist. Let your upper body and arms dangle for a count of ten. Straighten up slowly.

3. *Rest Break.* (You may bring a portable radio into the class.) Tell children: Put your head down on the desk. Close your eyes. Breathe regularly and deeply, in and out. Listen to soft music while remaining in this position. Pay attention to nothing but the music.

4. *Play* a game for fun!

5. *Remember* something that happened to you that made you very happy. Think about it. Talk about it to someone if you want.

6. *Talk* to someone in the family that you trust and if something worries you, tell him or her about it.

–4–

ACTIVITIES FOR GRADES 2–3

A. Parent Letter

B. *Activity Titles*   *Objectives*

4–1	Belonging	To identify the special groups to which one belongs.
4–2	Feeling Moods	To identify one's own feelings and the feelings of others.
		To practice ways to express feelings.
4–3	Seeking Help	To select responsible sources for help.
4–4	Making Choices	To become aware of the need to make choices in solving problems.
		To explore constructive ways to meet one's needs.
4–5	Peer Influences	To become aware of peer influences upon one's feelings.
4–6	Feeling Good	To become aware of and be able to choose ways of feeling good.
4–7	Need for Rules	To become aware of the need for rules in living.
4–8	Advertising	To explore the effects of advertising on us all.
4–9	Safety Rules for Dangerous Household Substances	To learn the possible dangers of ordinary household substances.
4–10	Medicines	To discuss the use and abuse of medicines.
4–11	Cigarette Smoking	To identify some of the harmful effects of smoking cigarettes.
4–12	Alcohol Is a Drug	To identify some of the effects resulting from drinking alcohol.

Dear Parent,

Activities for second and third grade students have been prepared, based on sound principles of growth and development, to positively influence your child in forming healthy ways to deal with one's self and others. Addressing these issues *prior* to the time when alcohol and other drug use is most likely to occur increases the probability that your child will not yield to those pressures that frequently lead to substance abuse. These activities will help your child to

1. Identify the special groups to which he or she belongs.
2. Identify one's own feelings and the feelings of others, and practice ways to express those feelings.
3. Select responsible sources for help.
4. Become aware of the need to make choices in solving problems, and explore constructive ways to meet their needs.
5. Become aware of peer influences upon one's feelings.
6. Become aware of and be able to choose healthy ways of feeling good.
7. Become aware of the need for rules in living.
8. Explore the effects of advertising on us all.
9. Learn of the possible dangers of ordinary household substances.
10. Discuss the use and abuse of medicines.
11. Identify some of the harmful effects of smoking cigarettes.
12. Identify some of the effects resulting from drinking alcohol.

We cannot protect our children from facing many of the problems of growing up in today's society, but we can prepare them for this task. Your interest, support, and caring interaction will assist your child in arriving at healthy attitudes and skills.

_____
Teacher

4–1

BELONGING

Objective

To have the children identify the special groups to which they belong. The children will explore their relationships with others in these groups.

Purpose

To develop a positive self-image.
To increase the sense of belonging and community.

Activities

Discuss the groups to which the children may belong in their order of "closeness" or intimacy.

1. Discuss belonging to one's own "special" family.
   a. Ask the children to complete the "Mystery Cruise" activity sheet (4–1A). Invite their families for a mystery trip. Draw a picture of each family member on the boat.
   b. Tell the children to write the name of their family on the flag on the "Family Flag" activity sheet (4–1B). Draw a picture on it telling something special about their family. Color the flag and cut it out. Paste it on the top of the boat. Talk about the fun they may have on the imaginary voyage. (Encourage fantasizing.)
   c. Discuss other things their family does together. What activities do they enjoy most? What activities are not much fun?

Note: Accept all of the students' statements as valid.

---

   d. Cut out pictures from magazines or newspapers of families doing things together.
2. Discuss having friends. Ask the children to:
   a. Help make a list of words that describe a friend.
   b. Tell a story about their best friend.
   c. Complete open-ended sentences:

Examples:

When I am with my friend I feel _____.

When I am a new person in a group I feel _____.

On the playground I feel _____.

Sharing makes me feel _____.

d. Discuss how to make new friends. Ask the children to role-play talking to a new child with whom they want to become friends.

3. Discuss belonging to a particular school.

   a. Talk about things that are fun at school. Talk about things that are not fun at school. Talk about other adults in the school environment: teachers, cafeteria workers, librarians, custodians, crossing guards, and so on.

   b. Complete the "Recess Fun" activity sheet (4–1C). Ask the children to draw their friends playing in the school playground. Talk about playing with friends at school.

4. Ask the children to which other groups they belong: place of worship, sports teams, dance classes, play groups, and so forth.

Reminder:

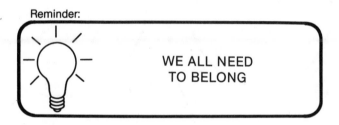

WE ALL NEED
TO BELONG

Name _____

Date _____

Mystery Cruise

1. Draw pictures of your family on the boat.
2. Color the pictures.

Family Flag

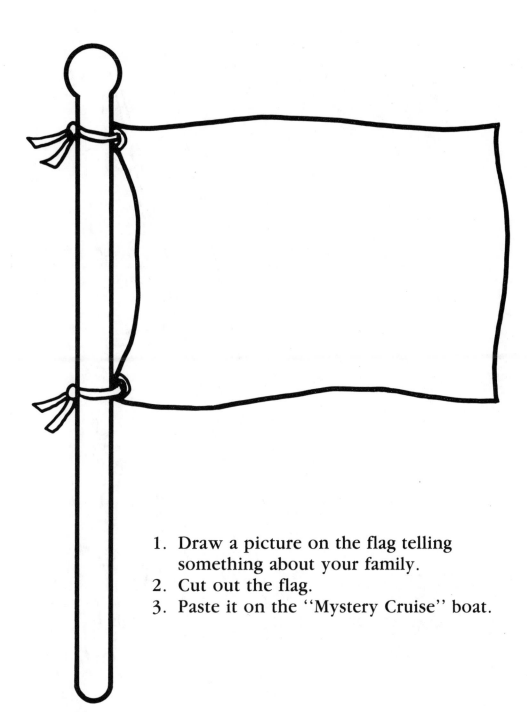

1. Draw a picture on the flag telling something about your family.
2. Cut out the flag.
3. Paste it on the "Mystery Cruise" boat.

Name _____

Date _____

Recess Fun

Draw three friends you play with during recess.

4–2

FEELING MOODS

Objective

To help the children begin to identify their own feelings and the feelings of others. The children will practice different ways to express feelings.

Purpose

To develop a positive self-image.
To clarify values and activities.
To improve personal communications.

Activities

1. To identify and discuss feelings:
   a. Write the names of the four feeling groups on the board. Put a number next to each feeling: (1) glad/happy, (2) mad/angry, (3) sad/depressed, (4) scared/afraid. "Feeling Faces" are shown on the activity sheet (4–2A).
   b. Write just the number on small pieces of paper for each child in the class. (Add more papers with numbers 2 and 3 as these emotions are most often expressed differently and may be misinterpreted.) Fold the papers to conceal the numbers.
   c. Pass out the secret paper to each of the students.
   d. Have the student act out the emotion number on the card for the rest of the group, so they can guess the feeling.
   e. Discuss the different expressions by the students of the same emotion.

> *Note: Explain to the students that it is helpful for them to ask questions about the "feelings" they see to avoid misunderstandings. For instance, a parent worried about finances or a teacher concerned about personal problems may show "mad" or "sad" feeling faces when responding to the child on other issues. By asking, "Are you mad at me?" or "You look sad," the child may receive a response that will clarify the situation and prevent feelings of isolation.*

   f. The child may choose a feeling and create a brief story about it to be shared with the class.
2. Use music to:
   a. Create an emotion: *Example:* a happy marching song.
   b. Identify some popular songs which speak of a particular feeling.

3. Have the students make a mask from a paper bag or paper plate (see the "Masks" activity sheet, 4–2B) to show how they feel today. (Encourage use of imagination.) They may put the mask on and act out the emotion without using words. (Encourage the use of all body parts.)

4. Ask the children to finish the following statements:

   a. I feel important when _____.

   b. I feel lonely when _____.

   c. When someone hurts my feelings I feel _____.

   d. When I break something I feel _____.

   e. When my mother scolds me I feel _____.

   f. When my best friend is not home when I call, I feel _____. (Accept all feelings as valid.)

5. Discuss visual and descriptive phrases used to express and explain emotion.

   Examples: mad/angry—"letting off steam"
                       "blowing my stack"
                       "blowing my cool"

   glad/happy—"happy as a lark," and so on.

6. Discuss the picture in the "Letting Off Steam" activity sheet (4–2C). Ask the children:

   a. What feeling, mood, or emotion do you *see*?

   b. What do you think is happening *inside* of the person?

   c. What do you think happens if you *keep feelings inside* all of the time? (Equate the build-up of pressure to a whistling tea kettle. When the top or spout cover is removed, it releases pressure by "letting off steam.")

   d. Name some things you can do to *safely* "let off steam" (talk to a family member, a friend, or a trusted adult; cry; play an active game that is fun).

7. Ask the children to observe how they react to happy news. (Encourage them to react spontaneously.) If you told them that they would have a day off from school tomorrow, how would they feel? How would they express the feelings? (A display of happy excitement is expected.) Now ask the students to listen to the same news and *not* react at all. Would it be hard *not to show* or express the good feelings? Will he or she have to "let out" the feeling soon to be more comfortable?

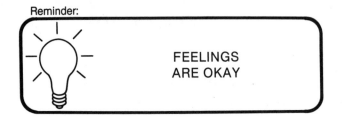

Reminder:

FEELINGS ARE OKAY

Feeling Faces

1   HAPPY

3   SAD

2   MAD

4   SCARED

Masks

Use

1. paper bag from the grocery store
2. marking pens or crayons

Directions

1. Draw how you feel on the paper bag.
2. Cut out holes for your eyes.

Use

1. paper plate
2. stapler or paste
3. marking pens or crayons
4. tongue depressor

Directions

1. Draw how you feel on the paper plate.
2. Staple or glue the tongue depressor to the plate.

Name _____

Date _____

Letting Off Steam

Compare the two pictures. How do you think the child feels?
What can the child do to feel better?

_____

_____

_____

_____

_____

4–3

SEEKING HELP

Objective

To help the children learn to select responsible sources for help.

Purpose

To improve decision-making and coping skills.
To clarify attitudes and values.

Activities

1. Discuss places to go for things one needs
   a. To fix a car (garage)
   b. To get dessert for supper (supermarket, bakery)
   c. To borrow books to read for fun (library)
2. Talk about people who are trained to provide certain kinds of help
   a. In case you get sick (doctor, nurse)
   b. To learn to spell (teacher)
   c. If someone is very sad; if someone drinks too much and you are worried (clergyman, counselor, school nurse)
3. Have the children "Find the Helpers" by matching the pictures shown in the activity sheet (4–3A).
4. Discuss how to call for help in the case of an emergency. Make a list of emergency numbers from the telephone directory that includes police department, fire department, ambulance, and so forth. Use a play phone to practice calling the numbers for an "invented" emergency. Remind students to give their *name, address,* and *type of emergency.*
5. Have the children close their eyes and think for a minute about a problem they had. What did they do about it? Whom did they ask for help? They may share the information with the class.
6. Talk about one's feelings when asking for help: Is it hard to ask adults (other than parents) for help when we need it? Why? Have you ever been too scared to ask for help? What happened?

> *Note: Reinforce the idea that we all need help sometimes. You may share a story with the students about a time you had to ask for help.*

7. Talk about getting help with "feeling" problems:

   Examples: What if . . .

   a. someone felt guilty and uncomfortable because he or she cheated on a test?

   b. someone felt sad because he or she had no friends?

   c. someone was angry with his or her brother or sister?

   d. someone got a bad mark on a test in school?

      What would the students want the "helper" to do for them? Would they want the "helper" to: listen, care, not judge, understand, give support, still like them anyway?

8. Have the children name three loving, caring people they know whom they could ask for help if they needed it.

Reminder:

I CAN ASK
FOR HELP

Find the Helpers

Draw a line from the problem to its helper.

4–4

MAKING CHOICES

Objective

To help the children become aware of the need to make choices in solving problems. They will explore constructive ways to meet their needs.

Purpose

To improve decision-making abilities.
To clarify attitudes and values.

Activities

1. Write a *problem* on the blackboard that the class may presently be experiencing, i.e., too much noise, playground activity is too rough, etc.

   a. List the *solutions* suggested by the class. Discuss the many *alternatives.* Discuss the *consequences* of each alternative.

   b. The class may *choose* one of the solutions to deal with the problem. (Stress the idea that there are *many ways* a problem can be solved.)

2. Explore the following problems with the steps described above.

   Examples: What if . . .

   a. You forgot your lunch money today. Would you

      (1) borrow money from the teacher?

      (2) go without lunch?

      (3) call home to ask your mother to bring in your lunch?

      (4) share a friend's lunch?

   b. You found a wallet containing $10.00 with the owner's name in it. Would you

      (1) keep the wallet and the money?

      (2) give it to a policeman?

      (3) throw away the wallet and keep the money?

      (4) leave it there?

      (5) have an adult help contact the owner to return it?

   c. You are playing at a friend's house. He or she asks you during the course of the visit to try one of the pills in the medicine cabinet just to see what would happen. Would you

(1) take one with your friend to try it?

(2) find an excuse to leave so you could go home?

(3) make believe you took it and throw it away so you could still be friends?

(4) tell him or her "*no, I don't want to take one.* It may make me sick."?

Create more problems to explore. Have the children role-play some solutions. Each child may choose his or her own solution.

3. Do the "Crossing the Stream" activity sheet (4–4A). Ask the students to "get to the other side of the stream" without getting their "feet wet." Encourage creativity and imagination. Possible solutions that can be drawn into the picture include adding stones, a plank, a rope on a tree, wading boots, and any other ideas the children may come up with as solutions.

Reminder:

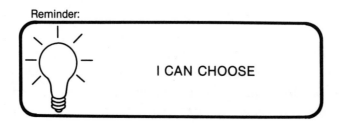

I CAN CHOOSE

4–4

MAKING CHOICES

Objective

To help the children become aware of the need to make choices in solving problems. They will explore constructive ways to meet their needs.

Purpose

To improve decision-making abilities.
To clarify attitudes and values.

Activities

1. Write a *problem* on the blackboard that the class may presently be experiencing, i.e., too much noise, playground activity is too rough, etc.
    a. List the *solutions* suggested by the class. Discuss the many *alternatives*. Discuss the *consequences* of each alternative.
    b. The class may *choose* one of the solutions to deal with the problem. (Stress the idea that there are *many ways* a problem can be solved.)

2. Explore the following problems with the steps described above.

    Examples: What if . . .

    a. You forgot your lunch money today. Would you
        (1) borrow money from the teacher?
        (2) go without lunch?
        (3) call home to ask your mother to bring in your lunch?
        (4) share a friend's lunch?

    b. You found a wallet containing $10.00 with the owner's name in it. Would you
        (1) keep the wallet and the money?
        (2) give it to a policeman?
        (3) throw away the wallet and keep the money?
        (4) leave it there?
        (5) have an adult help contact the owner to return it?

    c. You are playing at a friend's house. He or she asks you during the course of the visit to try one of the pills in the medicine cabinet just to see what would happen. Would you

(1) take one with your friend to try it?

(2) find an excuse to leave so you could go home?

(3) make believe you took it and throw it away so you could still be friends?

(4) tell him or her "*no, I don't want to take one. It may make me sick.*"?

Create more problems to explore. Have the children role-play some solutions. Each child may choose his or her own solution.

3. Do the "Crossing the Stream" activity sheet (4–4A). Ask the students to "get to the other side of the stream" without getting their "feet wet." Encourage creativity and imagination. Possible solutions that can be drawn into the picture include adding stones, a plank, a rope on a tree, wading boots, and any other ideas the children may come up with as solutions.

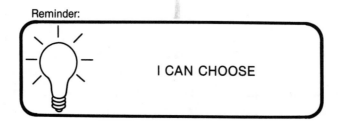

Reminder:

I CAN CHOOSE

Name _____

Date _____

Crossing the Stream

Find a way to cross the stream without getting your feet wet.

4–5

PEER INFLUENCES

Objective

To help the children become aware of their effect on others. They will also become more aware of peer influences upon their own feelings.

Purpose

To develop a positive self-image.
To improve decision-making skills.
To clarify values and attitudes.

Activities

1. Using a blackboard, have the students assist you in writing something good about each member of the class. Discuss how it makes the students feel when someone says something good about them. Discuss the importance of *accepting* these good statements.

2. Ask the children to each make a "personal poster" using the "shadow silhouette" technique. Here is an example:

   a. Have half the class members write their names on a piece of paper. Fold the papers and put them in a container.

   b. Have the other half of the class members pick a name from the container to form a "partnership."

c. Direct each child to cut words and pictures out of magazines and news-papers that tell the *positive* things that they believe to be true about their "partner."

d. Paste the words within the silhouette. Fill up all the space.

Note: You may have extra words cut out to assist the child who has dif-ficulty in finding enough good things to say.

---

3. Discuss feelings you might have if:

   a. Everyone in the class laughed at you when you made a mistake.

   b. You were left out of a game.

   c. Someone said something good about you.

   d. Someone tried to persuade you to do something you really did not want to do.

4. Play the "Telephone Game": Sit in a circle. Exclude one student from the cir-cle. Whisper a secret to a student who will then pass it to the next child, and so on, around the circle. (The group should not share the secret with the child who was excluded for half an hour.) Ask the excluded student: How did it feel being the only one who didn't know the secret? (The exercise should be re-peated several times so that other children can see how it feels to be left out.) Start a discussion about feeling lonely. (Be sure all children who have partici-pated in being left out now know the secret. Help them to feel comfortable back in the group.)

Reminder:

I AM UNIQUE

4–6

FEELING GOOD

Objective

To help children become aware of and be able to choose ways of feeling good.

Purpose

To improve coping skills.
To clarify attitudes and values.

Activities

> *Note: Give permission for the children to have "bad" feelings some-times. Encourage them to find someone that they trust to whom they can "give it away." Reinforce that feelings are neither right nor wrong and that we are only responsible for our behavior.*

1. Talk about the following questions, encouraging recognition of specific *body sensations* and *emotional feelings.* Ask:

   a. How do you feel (physically and emotionally), when you "feel good?"
   b. How do you feel (physically and emotionally), when you "feel bad?"
   c. Is it normal to "feel bad" sometimes?

   (You may share with the students that you "feel bad" sometimes, too.)

2. Have the children cut out pictures of activities from magazines or newspapers that they think would make them feel good. (*Examples:* a new game, their favorite desserts, vacation sites.) They may also choose to draw things of nature, such as flowers, the sun, the beach, or a picture of someone they like.

3. Have the children each make a desk plaque (shown on page 71) identifying something that makes them feel good. Stand it on their desk for the day so they may share the information with their classmates. Do other children share their interests? Allow time for dialogue related to information obtained through this exercise.

Directions for Making Desk Plaque

Cut out pieces of cardboard, oaktag, or construction paper approximately 8″ × 10″. Fold them in half lengthwise. Have the students print their names on it.

The children may either draw pictures or cut out pictures that show something that makes them feel good. Paste them onto their desk plaque.

4. Have the students write stories or draw pictures about something that made them feel bad today. Ask: What did you do about it? Name three or four solutions to help you feel better.

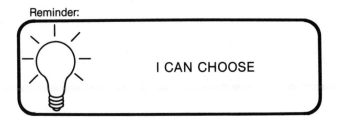

4–7

NEED FOR RULES

Objective

To help the student become aware of the need for rules to prevent problems.

Purpose

To improve decision-making ability.
To clarify personal values and attitudes.

Activities

1. Discuss some rules and why they were made. Role-play what would happen if:
   a. At home everyone came late for dinner?
   b. At school some children didn't leave the building during a fire drill?
   c. In the community everyone crossed at a red light?
2. Choose five or more children. Give them a ball. Observe how long it takes for rules to be needed so that each child gets his or her fair chance at participating in play.
3. Ask a child to play a game he or she likes to play with several other children who are unfamiliar with the game (board games may be used). But no one is allowed to tell them how to play. What happens? Are rules helpful? Why?
4. List some rules of good health to prevent problems.

   Examples: Brush your teeth after meals, get eight to ten hours of sleep at night, etc.
5. Ask the children to do the "No Swimming" activity sheet (4–7A).
   a. Connect the numbers.
   b. Discuss:
      (1) What is happening to the boy?
      (2) Why did he get into trouble?
      (3) How could he have enjoyed swimming and remained safe?
      (4) Talk about the need to follow rules and think of the consequences before one does something.
6. The following exercise will require the use of two to four small toy cars. Use a large piece of cardboard or oaktag. Draw lines on it to create streets. Decorate this "neighborhood" with houses and trees, as shown on the next page.

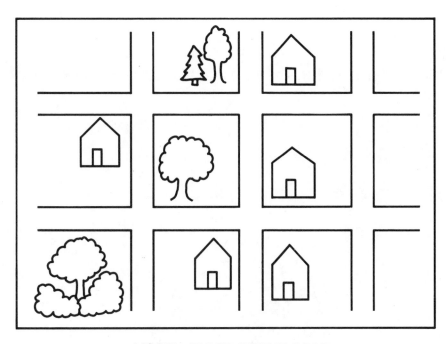

MODEL: RULES OF THE ROAD

a. Have several children "drive their cars" along the street any way they choose. Ask: What did you observe? Were there any accidents?

b. Ask the class to create rules of safety to prevent accidents.

c. Have them make street signs or issue the safety rules in a "government newsletter to the citizens."

d. Drive the cars on the roads with street signs. Ask: What do you observe now? Do rules help promote safety?

Reminder:

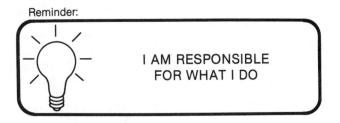

I AM RESPONSIBLE
FOR WHAT I DO

Name _____

Date _____

No Swimming

1. Connect the dots.
2. Color the picture.
3. On the back of this sheet, explain what is happening to the child. Why?

4–8

ADVERTISING

Objective

To have the children explore the effects of advertising.

Purpose

To improve decision-making ability.
To clarify personal values and attitudes.

Activities

1. Have the children:

   a. Make a collage of *positive* health-related products cut from old magazines. Discuss how the products add to our good health.

   b. Make a collage of products advertised that are not good for our health or are not for children (cigarettes, alcohol, diet pills, sleeping pills, and so forth).

2. Discuss the difference between *needing* something and *wanting* it. Collect pictures of things one may need and of things one may want. Ask: Where did you first see some of the things you want? (Explore the ads on TV, newspaper, and magazines, to make the children aware of the influence and appeal of the media.)

3. Ask the children: Were you ever disappointed after getting something that you had ordered after seeing it in an ad? Talk about it. Was the ad totally honest?

4. Discuss a favorite advertisement. What do you like about it?

5. Ask the children to create an ad about an imaginary product, using a "sales pitch" to sell it to the class. Were these ads totally honest?

Reminder:

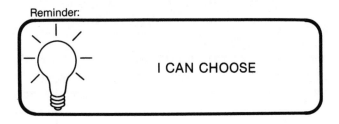

I CAN CHOOSE

4–9

SAFETY RULES FOR DANGEROUS
HOUSEHOLD SUBSTANCES

Objective

To have the children learn the possible dangers of ordinary household substances and learn the safety rules about them.

Purpose

To improve decision-making skills.
To promote good health practices.

Activities

Have the class:

1. List some household substances that can be dangerous if swallowed. These may include: hair dye, hair spray, nail polish, nail polish remover, drain and oven cleaner, cosmetics, lotions, furniture polish and cleaners, bleach, and so on.

2. Discuss the similarities and textures of substances that may look alike: salt, sugar, powdered bleach, flour, and some unlabeled medicines, for example: you may place some substances that look similar to each other into separate paper cups. *Do not label them* or tell the children what they contain. Ask the children to try to identify the substances. Talk about the dangers of using unknown substances. *Stress the importance of not tasting the substance to find out what it is!* Give them this reminder to follow: "When in doubt—throw it out!"

3. Collect some empty cartons and containers that have labels indicating that the contents were dangerous or poisonous. Show the children where to look for the labels that may display this important information.

> *Note: The cartons must be empty and cleaned out. It may be necessary for you to assume the responsibility of bringing in the containers, rather than having the children bring them, to ensure safety.*

4. To help the children recognize the warning labels for their own safety, have the students complete the "Warning Labels" activity sheet (4–9A) by tracing over the "warning" to complete them.

5. Read and study the information in the "Prevention Procedures" activity sheet (4–9B) regarding safety rules for dangerous substances. Discuss these rules in class. Have the children bring this activity sheet home to their parents.

6. Discuss the picture in the "Danger" activity sheet (4–9C). What is wrong with the picture? Have the children cross out things that are dangerous.

7. Ask the children to color the Fireman Red International Safety Sticker on the "Safety Message" activity sheet (4–9D) a bright red, and take the "Safety Message" home.

---

*Note: **Explain to your students that young children have difficulty in distinguishing between what is harmful and what is not, when bottles and containers are attractive to them. Because of this, this symbol was created to alert children** not **to** taste, touch *or* smell *anything that has this sticker on it.***

Have the children bring the parents' letter home, inviting them to send for the stickers. Suggest that the children assist parents in identifying and pasting the stickers on containers for dangerous substances. (The teacher or parent may choose to create their own labels or signs to paste on containers holding hazardous substances.)

8. Discuss the dangers of putting poisonous substances into containers originally used for other purposes. Give examples.

Reminder:

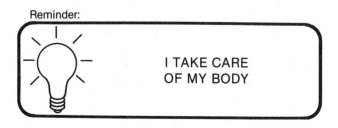

I TAKE CARE
OF MY BODY

Name _____

Date _____

Warning Labels

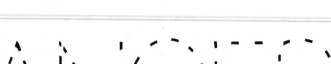

Trace the letters.

_____

**DO NOT TASTE, TOUCH, OR SMELL
ANYTHING WITH THESE LABELS.**

_____

Name _____

Date _____

Prevention Procedures
Household Safety Precautions
for Handling Dangerous Substances

1. Keep dangerous household substances (including hair dye, drain and oven cleaner, lotions, furniture cleaners, bleach, dishwasher detergent, gasoline products, etc.) out of the reach of children, either on high shelves or in locked cabinets.

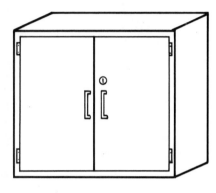

2. Designate one or two areas of the house for storing dangerous substances. Keep poisonous substances away from food items.

3. Keep all products in their original containers with their labels.

4. Keep weed killers, fertilizers, and insect sprays out of the reach of children. (These products can be absorbed by the skin.)

5. Be aware that swallowing cosmetics or perfumes can be deadly.

6. Keep medicines (including vitamins) labeled and out of the reach and sight of children.

7. Some indoor plants are toxic if ingested. Inquire at a florist which plants may be poisonous.

8. Liquor should be in a secure place, unavailable to children.

POISON CONTROL CENTER NUMBER: _____

Name _____

Date _____

Danger!

Put an X on the things in this picture that are dangerous for this baby.

Safety Message

Dear Parents:

Young children have difficulty identifying containers that hold dangerous or poisonous substances, like hair spray, furniture polish, and the like. The Fireman Red International Safety Sticker was designed to protect them, since this easy-to-recognize label will alert them *not* to touch, taste, or smell any container with this sticker on it.

We suggest that you allow your child to help you in placing these labels on hazardous substances.

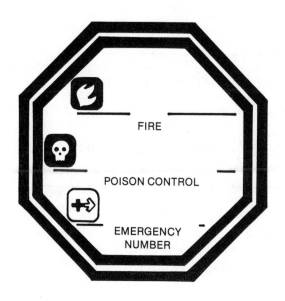

To order the Safety Stickers: Send $1.00 plus a legal size, self-addressed, stamped envelope to:

FIREMAN RED INTERNATIONAL SAFETY PROGRAM
DEPT. FC, P.O. BOX 1360
EVERGREEN, COLORADO 80439-1360

You will receive 24 safety labels, plus two telephone stickers to attach to or near your phone for emergency numbers.

4–10

MEDICINES

Objective

To discuss with the children the use and abuse of medicines (drugs).

Purpose

To improve decision-making skills.
To clarify personal values and attitudes.
To develop good health practices.

> *Note:* 1. *Repeat frequently to the students the fact that* only sick people need drugs.
> 2. *Use the word* drug *interchangeably with the word* medicine, *to reinforce the fact that all medicines contain drugs.*
> 3. *Make students aware that prescribed medicines may also be abused.*

Activities

1. Discuss the fact that drugs (medicines) *when used properly* help us to:
    a. Feel better when we are sick (aspirin, cough medicine)
    b. Keep well (vitamins)
    c. Prevent sickness (vaccines for flu and polio)
2. Talk about the different ways one can receive medicines (swallowing pills, liquid; injections; rubbing into the skin—ointments; inserting into the body orifices—suppositories).
3. Invite the children to talk about a time when they were ill. Did they need medicine? Did it make them feel better? Who gave the medicine to them?
4. Discuss from whom the child may accept medicines:
    a. Talk about the doctor's role, and his or her special skills.
    b. Talk about the nurse's role, and his or her special skills.
    c. Talk about the parent or other *designated* adult authority.
    d. May children take medicine by themselves?

e. May children take "medicine" from a friend or stranger who wants them to "try it"? Why not? Should you tell someone if that happens? Discuss. Make puppets and role-play.

Note: Reinforce to the children that they can say no.

---

5. Discuss:
   a. What children's medicine looks like (identifying pretty colors, attractive shapes); what it tastes like (identifying candylike or fruitlike tastes); what it smells like (identifying sweet and fruity smells that can be mistaken for candy).

Note: Stress that medicine is not *candy, even though they may look similar. You may demonstrate this with a piece of candy and a vitamin pill that look alike.*

---

   b. Why the makers of children's medicines made them look, smell, and taste so good.
6. Ask: If the doctor told your parent to give you one teaspoon of medicine, would two teaspoons make you better faster?
7. Ask where the medicines are kept in the children's homes. Discuss safety procedures, such as locked cabinets, child-proof covers, placing medicines out of children's reach).
8. Explore the role of the pharmacist/druggist with the children.

Reminder:

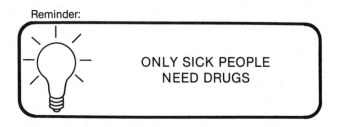

ONLY SICK PEOPLE NEED DRUGS

4–11

CIGARETTE SMOKING

Objective

To have the children identify some of the harmful effects of smoking cigarettes.

Purpose

To improve decision-making ability.
To clarify personal values and attitudes.

Activities

1. Ask the children to define the word, ''pollution.'' Webster's New Word Dictionary of the American Language gives this definition: ''Pol-lu-tion: to make *unclean*, impure, or corrupt; desecrate; defile; contaminate; *dirty*.''

2. Discuss pollutants in the air in the outside environment. Use pictures from magazines or newspapers. Include the pollution caused by factory smoke, car exhausts, rocket launches, smoke from *someone else's* burning cigarette, and so forth.

    a. Talk about how pollution makes the air ''dirty.''

    b. Have the children complete the ''Pollution Outside the Body'' activity sheet (4–11A).

3. Explain how all living things need air to breathe.

    Demonstrate:

    a. Put a plant under an airtight container. What begins to happen?

    b. Put ants or other insects in an airtight jar. Give them everything else they need to survive. What happens? Why? (When the ants' activity begins to decrease, open the jar and set them free.)

    c. Study the picture on the ''Pollution Inside the Body'' activity sheet (4–11B) that shows the passage of air into the lungs.

4. Talk about the fact that smoking cigarettes is harmful to our health, and how it ''pollutes'' the internal environment of our body (the lungs).

    a. Blow smoke from a cigarette through a tissue. (A smoking machine may be able to be obtained from your local Cancer Society or Heart Association.) What did you observe? Wouldn't that also make your lungs ''dirty?''

    b. What would happen to us if something interfered with our breathing properly? How long does it take to use up all the air in your lungs? Hold your breath and have someone check the time. Did you *have* to breathe very soon after you started holding your breath?

   c. Demonstrate the effects of sick or injured lungs:

      (1) Light a candle. Ask a child to stand a reasonable distance from the candle. Instruct the child to take a deep breath, and then blow out the candle.

      (2) Relight the candle. Ask the child to stand at the same distance from the candle. Instruct the child to take a deep breath and blow out at least half of the breath *before* attempting to blow out the candle. With the breath that is left, ask the child to blow out the candle. What happened?

5. Identify and discuss other facts about cigarettes and cigarette smoking:

   • Cigarettes are made of brown leaves called *tobacco.*

   • Tobacco contains a *drug* called *nicotine.*

   • Smoking cigarettes *deadens the nerve-endings for smell and taste.* People who smoke cannot smell or taste as well as nonsmokers.

   a. Look at the "Pollution Inside the Body" activity sheet (4–11B) again and find the nerve endings for smell. Find the nerve endings for taste on the tongue as shown in the activity sheet's illustration.

   b. People with stuffy noses cannot smell or taste well either. To simulate what it would be like for a smoker, ask a child to taste a snack. Then ask the child to hold his or her nose and taste the snack. Describe the difference. Ask other students to participate. A child can be asked to close his or her eyes, and hold his or her nose. Offer several different tasting foods. Have the child try to guess what foods are being offered. Discuss.

   • It makes the smoker's clothes and other things around him or her *smell.*

   • It *stains* the smoker's teeth.

   • It *costs* a lot of money to buy cigarettes.

6. Ask the children to create a poster illustrating the theme, "Smoking Is Dangerous for Your Health."

7. Have the students complete the "Danger! Warning! Caution!" activity sheet (4–11C). (You may read the incomplete sentences to the class.) The children can select the answer by word and picture to finish the sentence.

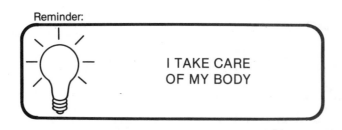

Reminder:

I TAKE CARE
OF MY BODY

Name _____

Date _____

Pollution Outside the Body

Fill in the missing letters of the things that dirty the air around us.

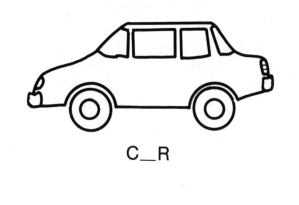

C_R

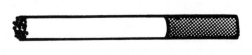

SM__K__NG

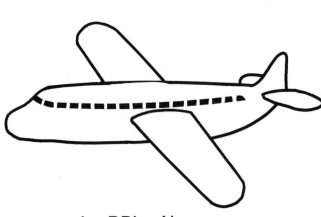

A__RPL__N__

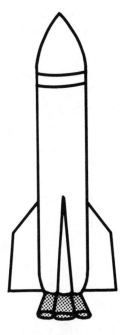

R__CK__T

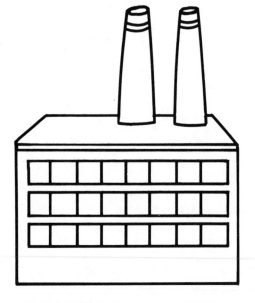

F_CT__RY

Name _____

Date _____

Pollution Inside the Body

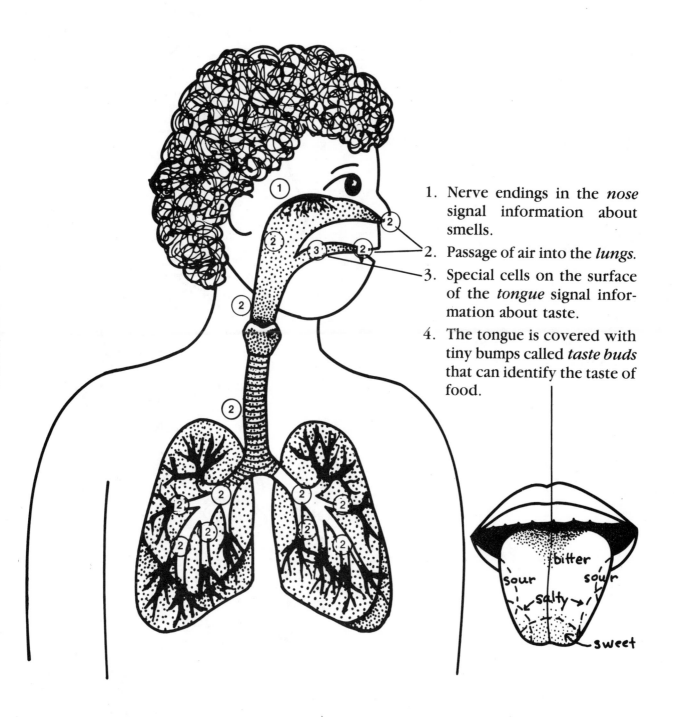

1. Nerve endings in the *nose* signal information about smells.

2. Passage of air into the *lungs*.

3. Special cells on the surface of the *tongue* signal information about taste.

4. The tongue is covered with tiny bumps called *taste buds* that can identify the taste of food.

Smoking cigarettes deadens the nerve-endings for smell and taste. People who smoke cannot smell or taste as well as nonsmokers.

Danger! Caution! Warning!

Complete the sentences by filling in the missing word.

Smoking cigarettes . . .

TEETH

1. costs a lot of _____.

LUNGS

2. makes it hard to smell and _____
   _____ food.

3. stains your _____.

NOSE

4. makes the smoker's _____
   smell.

TASTE

5. makes people _____.

CLOTHES

MONEY

6. makes your _____
   stuffy.

7. makes your _____ "dirty"
   so that it is hard to breathe.

SICK

4–12

ALCOHOL IS A DRUG

Objective

To have the children identify some of the effects which can result from drinking alcohol.

Purpose

To clarify personal attitudes and values.
To learn good health practices.

Activities

1. Discuss some times when adults may choose to use alcohol without causing problems (in moderation):

   a. Celebrations (weddings, bar mitzvah, Christian communion).

   b. With dinner to add to the enjoyment of the meal.

   c. Adding alcohol to food when cooking to add special flavor.

> *Note:* **Explain that alcohol (beer, wine, etc.) is not bad in itself, but it is the way that some adults may use it that can create bad problems and make one sick.**

---

2. Discuss unhealthy ways to drink alcohol:

   a. *Excessive use,* or "too much" alcohol.
   Review what happens when we have "too much" of anything: food, soda, sun. (Refer back to activity 3–7, "Setting Limits.") Ask: Have you ever seen anyone drunk? How did you know he or she was drunk? Could it be dangerous? Why? How do you feel, and what do you think when you see someone drunk?

   b. Drinking at the *wrong time* (while driving or operating dangerous equipment). Talk about the dangers that might be present when you can't keep your balance, focus your eyes, or coordinate your muscles. Have the children experience some of these feelings:

   Ask a student volunteer to

   (1) Cross his eyes and try to reach for an object.

   (2) Spin around in a safe place, with eyes closed, for about 15 seconds. Try to perform ordinary tasks when you are dizzy. What happens?

    c. Drinking *to change the way one feels* when one has uncomfortable feelings (mad, sad, scared) may become a habit. A person may not then learn to find other safer and healthier ways to "feel good."

3. Do adults have to drink to have a good time at a party? Talk about some fun you have had at a party recently. Can the class think of other ways to have fun when they are adults?

4. Explain that when some people drink too much they can get sick with a disease called *alcoholism*. They need help to get better. This disease also makes the people who love them unhappy. The alcoholic's family needs help also to be happy again.

   Tell the children that there are specially trained people and organizations available to offer help to alcoholics and their families. These are people one could see to talk to about "feeling" problems.

5. Complete the anagram in the "An Alcohol Word Search" activity sheet (4–12A).

6. Complete the "What Can Happen If Someone Drinks *Too Much* Alcohol" activity sheet (4–12B) by drawing a line to the "before" and "after" pictures. Encourage the students to create a "before" and "after" picture on the back of that sheet. Discuss the exercise with the class.

Reminder:

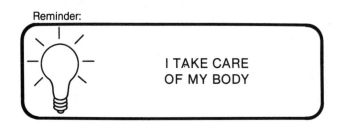

I TAKE CARE
OF MY BODY

An Alcohol Word Search

Tell about some times when adults may use and enjoy alcohol without getting sick.

Things to do to feel good:

1. in COOKING

3. at MEALTIME

1. RIDE

2. to CELEBRATE

4. at RELIGIOUS SERVICES

2. PAINT

3. PLAY BALL

Find and circle each word in the box below that is underlined in the above exercise. The words can be found horizontally, vertically, and diagonally.

```
T  M  C  O  O  K  L  S  P  B
L  R  E  L  I  G  I  O  U  S
P  I  L  A  C  M  Z  W  B  E
O  D  E  P  L  A  Y  G  R  R
S  E  B  R  O  T  S  E  J  V
O  U  R  A  P  A  I  N  T  I
B  O  A  C  M  T  E  M  Z  C
E  M  T  S  O  I  L  Q  E  E
F  T  E  N  G  J  M  D  L  S
L  R  N  E  B  A  L  L  H  K
```

What Can Happen if Someone Drinks Too Much Alcohol

Draw a line from each "before" picture to its "after" picture. Then make up your own "before" and "after" pictures on the back of this sheet.

–5–

ACTIVITIES FOR GRADE 4

A. Parent Letter

B. *Activity Titles*   *Objectives*

5–1	Self-Image and Expectations	To identify that the expectations and responses of other people influence how we see ourselves.
5–2	Self-Acceptance	To value one's own uniqueness and to accept ourselves as we are.
5–3	Problem Solving	To examine problem solving and practice decision making.
5–4	Needs Vs. Wants	To define and compare the difference between needs and wants.
5–5	Good Health = Responsible Choices	To become aware of the need to make responsible choices to maintain good health.
5–6	Prescription Drugs	To learn the proper use of prescription (drugs) medicines.
5–7	Nonprescription Drugs	To learn the proper use of nonprescription (drugs) medicines.
5–8	Forming Habits	To define the word ''habit'' and recognize how habits are formed.
5–9	Breaking Habits	To explore the difficulties experienced in breaking habits.
5–10	Dangerous Health Habits	To identify the difficulties in breaking unhealthy habits, and the need to make choices in the future to promote health.
5–11	''Smoking Is Dangerous to Your Health''	To recognize the serious health problems caused by smoking.
5–12	Attitudes About Alcohol	To identify some attitudes about alcohol.
5–13	Alcohol and Its Effects	To identify some of the effects of using the drug, alcohol.
5–14	Effects of ''Too Much'' Alcohol	To explore and demonstrate some of the effects of drinking too much alcohol.

Dear Parent,

Activities for fourth grade students have been prepared, based on sound principles of growth and development, to positively influence your child in forming healthy ways to deal with him- or herself and others. Addressing these issues *prior* to the time when alcohol and other drug use are most likely to occur increases the probability that your child will not yield to those pressures that frequently lead to substance abuse. These activities will help your child to

1. Identify that the expectations and responses of other people influence how we see ourselves.
2. Value his or her own uniqueness and to accept him- or herself as is.
3. Examine problem solving and practice decision making.
4. Define and compare the difference between needs and wants.
5. Become aware of the need to make responsible choices to maintain good health.
6. Discuss the proper use of prescription (drugs) medicines.
7. Discuss the proper use of nonprescription (drugs) medicines.
8. Define the word "habit" and explore the difficulties of breaking bad health habits.
9. Identify the health dangers of cigarette smoking.
10. Learn about the drug, alcohol, and its effects.

We cannot protect our children from facing many of the problems of growing up in today's society, but we can prepare them for this task. Your interest, support, and caring interaction will assist your child in arriving at healthy attitudes and skills.

_____
Teacher

5–1

SELF-IMAGE AND EXPECTATIONS

Objective

To help the children become aware that the expectations and responses of other people influence how we see ourselves.

Purpose

To develop a positive self-image.

Activities

1. Have each child ask a member of the family (preferably the mother or father) to write a "love letter" to him or her that mentions *specific* nice things about their child. It may be shared with the class if the student wishes. Suggest to the students that this letter be kept in a special place for them to read when they need to feel good about themselves.

2. Put the names of all the students in a hat.

   a. Have each student pick out one name and keep it a secret.

   b. Instruct the children to observe the general behavior of their "secret" classmate during the course of an ordinary school week.

   c. Instruct them to keep a diary of the good, kind, or helpful things they observe their "secret" classmate doing.

   d. On the last day of the week have the students identify their "secret" students and read the list of positive activities they observed.

   e. Make a folder with the information on it. Give it to the "secret" classmate to enjoy.

   f. Let the students talk about how he or she felt when their good acts were read aloud.

3. Have the class discuss the use of labels to identify things.

   a. Name some things that have labels on them (canned food, designer jeans, medicine bottles).

   b. What do labels tell us?

   c. Ask: Do we usually believe what the label tells us without checking?

   d. Use some words that people use to "label" other people (lazy, silly, slow, a sissy, etc.). Complete the "Label Cans, Not People" activity sheet (5–1A).

e. Do people believe these labels? Ask the children to think of someone who they know has a "label." Does the "label" affect how we treat the person? How do you think the person feels? Is the "label" always true?

4. Ask: Does anyone have a "nickname?" Who was the first person who used it for you? Why? Do you like it? Would you like to change it or stop using it? Why don't you?

Note: ***Children can assume the roles "assigned" to them by other people. Tell the childen that new nicknames can be chosen if desired to form a more positive self-image.***

Reminder:

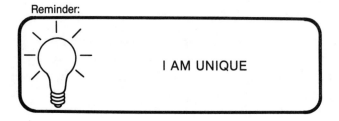

I AM UNIQUE

Name _____

Date _____

Label Cans, Not People

Unscramble the words below sometimes used to label people.

1. LZAY _____   6. UIDTPS _____

2. "KSIC" _____   7. RNED _____

3. ADB _____   8. RECEP _____

4. MUDB _____   9. OLSW _____

5. YRACZ _____   10. ISSSY _____

5-2

SELF-ACCEPTANCE

Objective

To help the children learn to value their own uniqueness, and to accept themselves as they are. They will become aware that they can grow by accepting challenges.

Purpose

To develop a positive self-image.
To clarify values and attitudes.

Activities

> *Note:* **With the class explore the idea that we should not compare ourselves to anyone else. We are unique. There are no two people exactly alike.**

1. To demonstrate the foolishness of comparisons, have the children compare each of the following: two colors, two pieces of fruit, two flavors of ice cream, two favorite movies.

   Example: Compare apples and oranges.

   a. Have the children tell how they are the same.

   b. Have the children tell how they are different.

   c. By a show of hands, take a vote to see which fruit each child *preferred*. (It is presumed that each fruit will receive votes.)

   d. Help the children to recognize that each fruit was voted for *because* it was either an apple or an orange. Each is unique, with its own desirable characteristics and its own limitations.

2. Complete the "My Treasure Chest" activity sheet (5–2A). Assist the children in focusing on their capabilities and accomplishments, including those functions that we may all take for granted.

   a. Direct each child to write a list of things that they *can do.* (*Suggestions:* I can—run, sing, wish, try, jump, swim, bake, listen, walk, write, ride a bike, paint, see, think, ski, help, etc.)

   b. They may write the words inside "The Treasure Chest."

   c. The children can add words to their "treasures" whenever they wish to focus on something that they *can do.*

3. Have the students complete the "Balancing It Out" activity sheet (5–2B).

   a. Make a list of their strengths and a list of their weaknesses/limitations.

   b. Discuss the process of recognizing a limitation as a *challenge* to overcome.

   c. Discuss physical feelings when facing a challenge (nervousness, jitters, sweating, feeling like "running"). Stress that *everyone* has weaknesses and limitations!

4. Explore these topics with the children:

   a. What would you do if someone laughed at you when you tried something new and could not do it very well?

   b. How would you feel?

   c. Would it discourage you from trying it again?

Note: Emphasize that most people don't do things well the first time. No one *does everything well—but* each *of us can do* something *well.*

---

5. Have the children begin doing something they used to be too "scared" to do, such as speaking in front of the class (try it!); playing a new game during recess (try it!); talking to a saleslady at a store (try it!).

   a. Ask each student to identify something he or she would like to do better, and write it on a piece of paper. Have each child keep a diary of progress.

   b. They may share their progress at the end of a week. (Offer appropriate support and encouragement with the class for each student.)

6. Direct the student to read biographies of people who overcame their special weaknesses/limitations to become more special, instead of "giving in" to them.

Reminder:

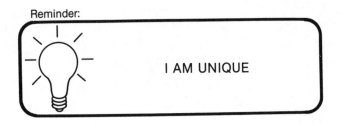

I AM UNIQUE

My Treasure Chest

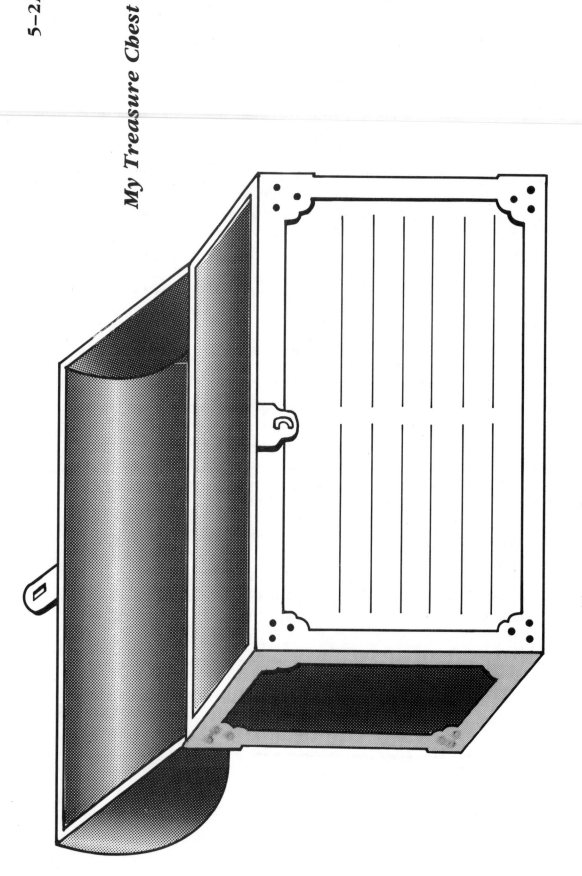

Treasures of _____

Name

Write things you can do in the treasure chest.

Balancing It Out

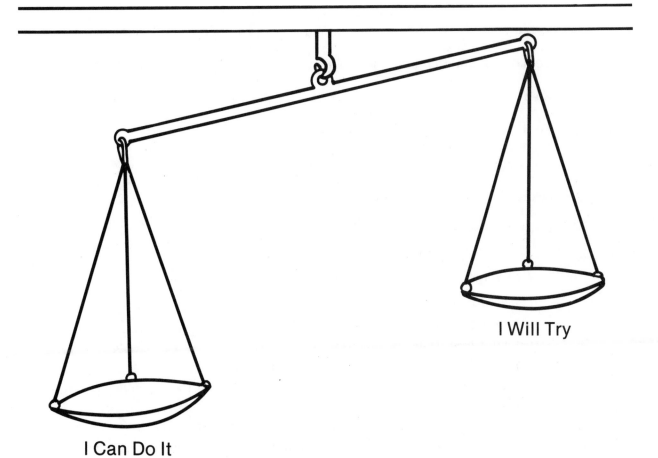

I Will Try

I Can Do It

THREE THINGS I CAN DO WELL

_____

_____

_____

TWO THINGS I WOULD LIKE TO DO BETTER

_____

_____

_____

5–3

PROBLEM SOLVING

Objective

To have the children examine problem solving and practice making decisions.

Purpose

To improve decision-making ability.
To improve coping skills.
To clarify personal attitudes and values.

Activities

1. Have the class:

   a. Choose a *problem* to explore as a *group*.

      Examples:

      (1) getting up late for school
      (2) losing a library book
      (3) your best friend just moved away
      (4) a student in a higher grade is bothering you

   b. List some of the consequences that may result from these problems. List *solutions*.

   c. Discuss *sources of help* in coping with these problems.

   d. Have *each* child make his or her own *decision* concerning the problem to add to the list.

   e. See how many *different* solutions there are to the *same* problem. (Accept all reasonable statements.)

2. Discuss with the students the fact that each decision will have consequences. Discuss the consequences of each decision. Is each child willing to accept them? Encourage the children to monitor the solutions they have chosen over a period of time. If they are not satisfied with the results, encourage them to try another solution.

3. Complete the "What Would You Do If . . ." activity sheet (5–3A).

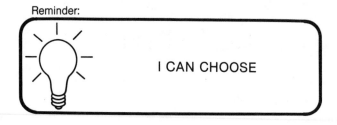

Reminder:

I CAN CHOOSE

What Would You Do If . . .

1. The crossing guard was not at the corner when you arrived:

   choices: 1. _____

                   2. _____

                   3. _____

   consequences: 1. _____

                   2. _____

                   3. _____

   decision: _____

2. The girl in front of you accidentally dropped her new gold pen. She was not aware of it. You are the only one around.

   choices: 1. _____

                   2. _____

                   3. _____

   consequences: 1. _____

                   2. _____

                   3. _____

   decision: _____

3. You stayed overnight at your friend's house. His parents are having a party. You go to the kitchen with your friend for cookies and milk. There are three glasses of unfinished drinks containing liquor on the counter. Your friend wants you to finish the drinks with him.

choices: 1. _____

               2. _____

               3. _____

consequences: 1. _____

               2. _____

               3. _____

decision: _____

4. Your friends want you to try smoking a cigarette with the group. You really do not want to try it.

choices: 1. _____

               2. _____

               3. _____

consequences: 1. _____

               2. _____

               3. _____

decision: _____

5. You have a bad headache. You are alone in the house. There are pills in the cabinet that your mother uses for her headaches.

choices:
1. _____
2. _____
3. _____

consequences:
1. _____
2. _____
3. _____

decision: _____

6. Your friends are smoking a "joint" of marijuana. They are passing it around in the group. It is your turn. You want to see what it is like, but you know your parents would be upset.

choices:
1. _____
2. _____
3. _____

consequences:
1. _____
2. _____
3. _____

decision: _____

5–4

NEEDS VS. WANTS

Objective

To have the children define and compare the difference between *needs* and *wants* and explore needs and wants in their own lives. They will discuss constructive ways of meeting their needs.

Purpose

To improve decision-making and coping skills.
To clarify personal values and attitudes.

> *Note: Refer back to Maslow's Hierarchy of Needs (see Figure 1–1). People may use drugs to escape the pain caused by unmet needs and desires (including security, self-esteem, love, and acceptance).*

Activities

Have the children:

1. Define "needs" (something *required*; something *essential* that is lacking).
2. Define "wants" (a *desire* or *wish* for something).
3. Have the students list five things they think they *need* (even if they already have them). Discuss what would happen if they didn't have them.
4. Have the children list five things they *want*. What would happen if they didn't have them?
5. Have the children research and give reports on children in other countries and cultures. What do they eat? What do they wear? What games do they play?
6. Are *needs* or *wants* the *same* all over the world? Distinguish between universal needs and what children of each culture may value and desire. Talk about cultural values and desires as something we learn.
7. List some things that influence what we want:
   a. Television—Do the advertisements appear to confuse needs and wants? Discuss specific advertisements.
   b. Peer Pressure—"Everyone has one."
   c. Social Pressure—Do children want to act grown up or rich?

8. Have the children complete the "Bright Balloons" activity sheet (5–4A). Identify *needs* by coloring the balloons *red*. Identify *wants* by coloring the balloons *blue*.

9. Ask the childen how they feel when they don't get what they want (jealous, angry, sad, embarrassed). How would they feel if they didn't get what they needed?

10. Have the children explore healthy and unhealthy ways of coping with those uncomfortable feelings.

Healthy	*Unhealthy*
admit your feelings	get even
talk to someone	hurt someone
play with friends	give up
ask for help	break things
ask for hugs	pretend you feel okay
exercise	use alcohol/drugs
	believe you are not okay

11. Use the following sentence to have the children recognize a feeling, the situation to which they are reacting, and how to cope with it.

<u>What</u>   <u>Why</u>   <u>How</u>

I feel _____ because _____. To make myself feel better, I will _____.

Example:

I feel <u>angry</u> because <u>Mary was chosen for the part in the play</u>. I will <u>admit my feelings and talk to someone about them</u> so I will feel better.

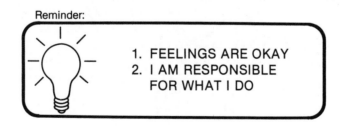

Reminder:
1. FEELINGS ARE OKAY
2. I AM RESPONSIBLE FOR WHAT I DO

Name _____

Date _____

Bright Balloons

Color RED each balloon that shows something everyone NEEDS.
Color BLUE each balloon that shows something we WANT.

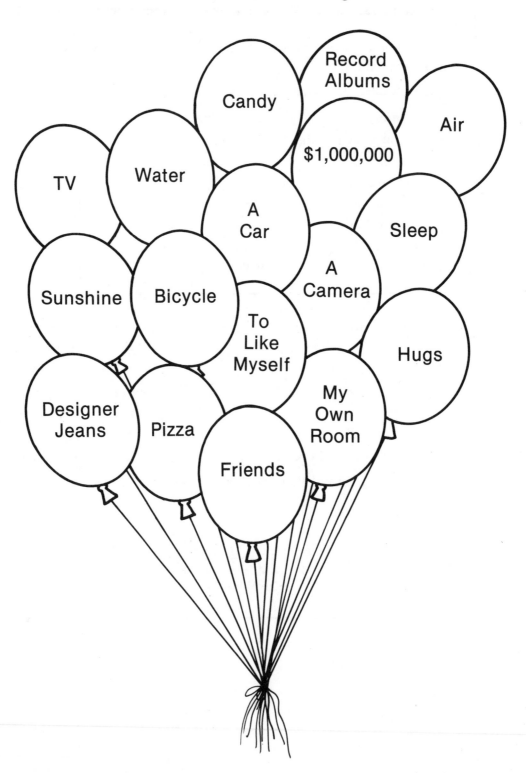

5–5

GOOD HEALTH = RESPONSIBLE CHOICES

Objective

   To have the children become aware of the need to use substances properly, and recognize the need to make responsible choices to maintain good health.

Purpose

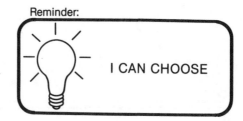

Reminder:

I CAN CHOOSE

   To assist in decision-making.
   To clarify personal attitudes and values.

Activities

> *Note: Emphasize to the class that substances are neither good nor bad in themselves. It is how people use them that makes the outcome good or bad.*

1. Ask the children to
   a. Examine the list of substances (see the activity sheet, 5–5A) found in the home, which are potentially dangerous when misused.
   b. Check where potentially harmful substances are stored in their homes.
   c. Discuss safe places and safe ways to store substances (in locked cabinets, away from food, out of the reach of children, in proper containers, tightly covered, properly labeled).

2. Ask the children to name some ways that substances can be misused. For example:
   a. For the wrong reason
   b. By the wrong person
   c. In the wrong amount
   d. At the wrong time to promote good health
   Give examples of each.

3. Discuss what to do in the event of an accidental poisoning. Have the children complete the "Emergency" activity sheet (5–5B).

4. Have the children:
   a. Complete the stories in the "Healthy Decisions" activity sheet (5–5C).
   b. Discuss what substance was involved.
   c. How could it have been misused in the situation?
   d. Talk about making responsible choices to maintain good health.

Name _____

Date _____

Products That Are Potentially Dangerous to Children in the Home

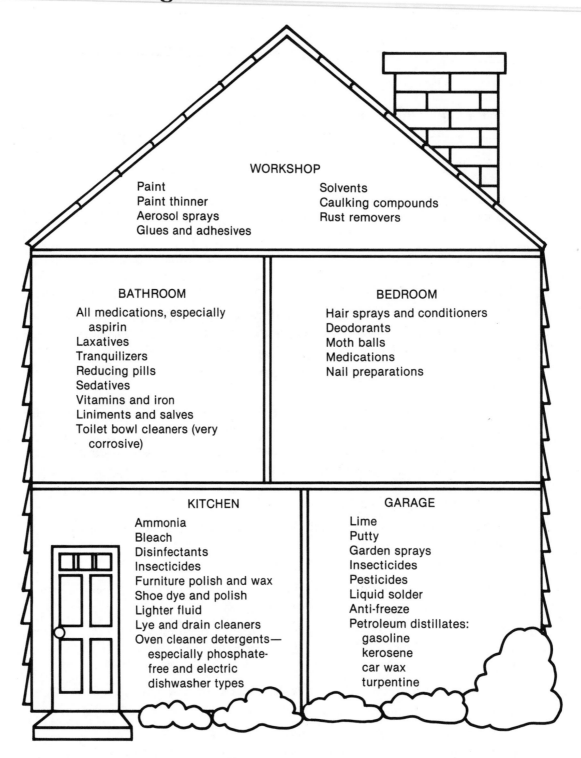

WORKSHOP
Paint
Paint thinner
Aerosol sprays
Glues and adhesives
Solvents
Caulking compounds
Rust removers

BATHROOM
All medications, especially
  aspirin
Laxatives
Tranquilizers
Reducing pills
Sedatives
Vitamins and iron
Liniments and salves
Toilet bowl cleaners (very
  corrosive)

BEDROOM
Hair sprays and conditioners
Deodorants
Moth balls
Medications
Nail preparations

KITCHEN
Ammonia
Bleach
Disinfectants
Insecticides
Furniture polish and wax
Shoe dye and polish
Lighter fluid
Lye and drain cleaners
Oven cleaner detergents—
  especially phosphate-
  free and electric
  dishwasher types

GARAGE
Lime
Putty
Garden sprays
Insecticides
Pesticides
Liquid solder
Anti-freeze
Petroleum distillates:
  gasoline
  kerosene
  car wax
  turpentine

Add other products you may have seen stored in your home. Have safety measures been taken?

Name _____

Date _____

Emergency!
If Accidental Poisoning Occurs . . .

1. KEEP CALM

2. CALL FOR HELP IMMEDIATELY

3. COLLECT EVIDENCE (bottles, pills, containers)

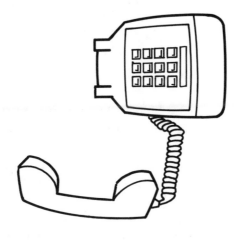

HOW

CALL FOR HELP: Tell your name.

Give your address.

Give your telephone number.

Give all important information.

Stay on the telephone to answer any further questions and to take directions.

WHO

Poison control center number: _____

Police or emergency number: _____

Doctor's number: _____

Dial "O" for operator to ask for help.

Healthy Decisions

Directions

    A. Complete the stories on another sheet of paper.
    B. What substance was involved?
    C. How could it have been misused in the situation?

----

1. John's parents are having a party and they will serve wine to their friends. John wants to drink a full glass of wine to see how he feels after the drink.

2. Mary is allergic to eggs and can become very sick if she eats anything with eggs in it. She knows the cake her mother has bought is made with eggs, but she wants a piece anyway.

3. Helen is beginning to have a weight problem. Sometimes she eats a lot of cake and candy when she feels lonely and unhappy, to make herself feel better.

4. Bob is very hungry when he comes home from school. He wants to finish the leftover meat-loaf in the refrigerator, but the meat smells "funny."

5. Mandy hurt her hand. She knows the dentist had given her brother medicine for pain when he had his tooth taken out. Maybe she can use that for her pain.

6. Michael's friend came over to his house after school. While they were fooling around, one of the boys started spraying hair spray in the faces of the other boys.

7. Donald is in the garage where his father is preparing to put the insecticide into the spray can. His father leaves the garage for a moment to answer the telephone. Donald wants to examine the solution.

8. Cheryl has a new baby sister. Her mother is busy in the kitchen. Cheryl wants to put powder on the baby so she will smell nice. She takes a white powder that has no label on it, from the bathroom cabinet.

9. Ed is carrying an uncovered bottle of bleach to his sister, who is washing her blouse in the sink. Some of the bleach splashes up into Ed's eyes when he sets it down on the countertop.

10. Danny and Tom are playing in their room. They have decided to play that they are chemists. Both boys collect some cleaning solutions to mix together. They begin to feel dizzy and sick.

5–6

PRESCRIPTION DRUGS

Objective

To have children discuss prescription drugs (medicines).

Purpose

To increase drug knowledge.
To assist in decision making.

Activities

1. Ask the children to define the word "drug." (Any substance—liquid, powder, or solid—taken by mouth, inhaled, injected, or rubbed into the skin, that affects the way the body or the mind naturally works.)

2. Have the children define and discuss *prescription* drugs. (Medicines that, legally, can be purchased only on the order of a doctor or a dentist, a) for specific reasons, b) for a specific person, and c) prepared by a specially trained person called a pharmacist.)

3. Ask the children to talk about the last time they went to the doctor or dentist and were given medicine. What was the problem? What medicine was given? Did it make them feel better?

4. The teacher can bring in empty, clean bottles that once contained prescription medicines.

    a. Notice the label. It states the name of one particular person, the name of the medicine, the amount and time to be given, the name of the doctor, the date, the prescription number and number of refills if needed, the pharmacy's name, address, and phone number. Here are two examples:

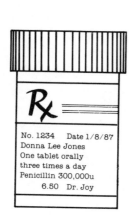

No. 1234   Date 1/8/87
Donna Lee Jones
One tablet orally
three times a day
Penicillin 300,000u
    6.50   Dr. Joy

No. 1234 Date: 6/23/88
Liz Buckley
Spray to affected
area for itching
as needed
    7:00 Dr. J. Walsh

b. Discuss some of the considerations the doctor makes before he can order your medication:

(1) age

(2) weight

(3) general health of the person

(4) severity of the condition

Note: A drug may affect different people in different ways.

5. Have the children make reports on the discovery of drugs (medicines) that have helped mankind (measles vaccine, polio vaccine, penicillin, and so forth).

Note: Stress that medicine may be taken only under the supervision of a parent, physician, nurse, or specific designated adult.

6. List some safety rules for using prescription medication with the children. (See the "Safety Rules for Prescription Drugs" activity sheet, 5–6A.) The students may take this activity sheet home to review with their parents.

Reminder:

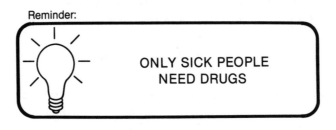

ONLY SICK PEOPLE
NEED DRUGS

Safety Rules for Prescription Drugs

Dr. P. Smith

2357 PINEBROOK TPK
OLDHAM, N.J. 10251

555–7890
555–7897

For_____ Date _____

 SAFETY RULES FOR TAKING MEDICINES

1. Take the medicine as directed.
2. Finish the entire prescription.
3. Discard any unused medicines.
4. Never share your medicines with anyone else.
5. Keep medicine in a safe place, out of the reach of children.
6. Keep medicines in their original container.
7. Do not take several medicines at the same time, unless the doctor is aware of *all* of them.
8. Mixing drugs (medicines) and alcohol can be fatal.
9. Never describe medicine as ''candy.''
10. Never give medicines in the dark.
11. Never give medicine from an unlabeled container.
    WHEN IN DOUBT—THROW IT OUT.

Refill _____ X _____ **M. D.**

5–7

NONPRESCRIPTION DRUGS

Objective

To have children discuss nonprescription medicines.

Purpose

To increase drug knowledge.
To assist in decision making.

Activities

1. Define the term nonprescription drugs. (Medicines that do not require a doctor's order, or the assistance of a pharmacist. They can be found on open shelves in a drug store or a supermarket.)

2. Have the children check the shelves in those stores and report the names of some drugs that they find. Ask them to read the labels and list:

   a. The name of the product.

   b. The condition for which it is to be used.

   c. Whether it is a liquid, tablet, or capsule.

   d. Any warnings or cautions listed.

   Were there other products on the shelf which could be used for the same condition?

3. Have the children report on two TV advertisements dealing with nonprescription medication (aspirin, cold preparations, antacid preparations, etc.). Does the medicine always seem to make the people better and happier? Can that be true always? Why would the manufacturer want people to believe that? Are they always completely honest? Compare ads for brands of aspirin. Can they *all* be the best?

4. List three substances which are socially acceptable, contain a drug, and can be bought in supermarkets.

   a. Cigarettes (tobacco containes *nicotine*).

   b. Coffee, tea, cocoa, cola (these contain *caffeine*).

   c. beer, wine, whiskey (these contain *alcohol*).

5. Have the children name conditions for which one could buy nonprescription medicine (drugs) in our society.

   Examples:

to fall asleep	for an upset stomach
to wake up	for a cold
to lose weight	for muscle pain
to gain weight	for a toothache
to relieve headaches	to relieve back pain

   Name a product for each condition.

6. Have the children:

   a. List three ways to get rid of a headache instead of taking medicine.

      Examples:

      (1) rest

      (2) exercise

      (3) play

   b. List three ways to fall asleep instead of taking sleeping pills.

      Examples:

      (1) warm milk

      (2) more daily activity

      (3) talk to someone

   c. List three ways to lose weight instead of taking diet pills.

      Examples:

      (1) eat low-calorie food

      (2) exercise

      (3) don't snack between meals

   Reminder:

   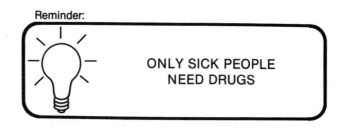

   ONLY SICK PEOPLE
   NEED DRUGS

5–8

FORMING HABITS

Objective

To have the children discuss what a *habit* is and how it develops.

Purpose

To improve decision-making skills.
To clarify personal values and attitudes.

Activities

1. Have the children
   a. Define the word "habit."
   b. Define the word "automatic."
      (It is an *activity done without thinking*; an *automatic* spontaneous response, developed by *repetition*.)

2. Have the children list some good health *habits*: brushing one's teeth, washing one's hands before meals, seeing the dentist once or twice a year.
   Have the children also list some unhealthy *habits*: biting one's nails, overeating, staying up too late.

3. Ask: Are there particular things you do "automatically" when you are afraid or tired, to make yourself more comfortable or at ease (bite your nails, eat something sweet, stroke your hair)? Do you always know when you are doing that? (The children may need help in identifying some of these comforting habits.)

4. Talk about how activities can develop into habits.

   Examples:

   a. Frequent reminders from concerned people.
   b. It feels good to do it.
   c. It's hard to stop doing it.
   d. We don't think of the consequences.

5. Ask: Do you remember which sock or shoe you put on first this morning? Is it done the same way each day without thinking about it? Try to change your usual pattern and do it differently each morning for a few days. Were you uncomfortable? Did it take more time to get dressed when you had to think about it? Did that make you feel uncomfortable and irritable?

5–9

BREAKING HABITS

Objective

To have the children explore the difficulties of breaking habits.

Purpose

To improve coping skills.
To clarify personal values and attitudes.

Activities

1. Request that the children try to give up something for a week that is very important to each of them. Examples could be salt or sugar on food, watching a favorite television program, eating candy, etc.

2. Have the children keep a record of their experiences. The teacher will review the directions for the daily diary with the children as shown in the example below. These directions are also to be used for the "Loosening the Chain" activity sheet (5–9A). The children will include the coded information to tell their stories.

Directions for "Loosening the Chain"

1. To list the number of times you forgot, add the __number__ and __T__ to indicate how many times.

2. To tell what kind of feelings you had each day when you were stopping a habit, use the following signs:

good ☺   bad ◣

okay ☐   very bad ■

3. To show if you decided to *quit* the activity, use ✔ for *yes*; and an X to indicate *no*.

4. Add any additional information you wish.

Examples:

Habit: <u>EATING CAKE</u>

AM	AFTERNOON	PM
Monday 1. *1T*	1. *OT*	1. *2T*
2. ☺	2. ☺	2. ◩
3. ✕	3. ✕	3. ✕
4. *none*	4. *none*	4. When I am tired it's harder

This diary indicates that the student had one piece of cake on Monday morning, felt good, decided to continue the activity, and did not wish to add any information to the page.

On Monday afternoon, the student did not eat any cake, felt good, decided to continue the activity, and did not wish to add any information to the page.

On Monday evening, the student had two pieces of cake, felt bad, decided to continue the activity, and in the <u>additional information</u> part, added a why, i.e., "When I am tired, it is harder to be successful in breaking a habit."

3. Explore some of the feelings that occur when one tries to break a habit. Ask: Was it hard to do? How did it feel when you couldn't have what you wanted, or do what was "automatic" before? Were you uncomfortable? What did you do about it? Did you give up trying? If you did give up trying, did you feel like you had failed? Did you feel unhappy with yourself?

Reminder:

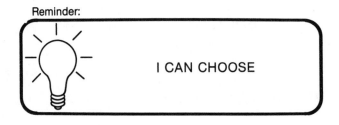

I CAN CHOOSE

Date _____

Loosening the Chain—
Daily Diary

HABIT: _____

	MORNING	AFTERNOON	EVENING
MONDAY	1. 2. 3. 4.	1. 2. 3. 4.	1. 2. 3. 4.
TUESDAY	1. 2. 3. 4.	1. 2. 3. 4.	1. 2. 3. 4.
WEDNESDAY	1. 2. 3. 4.	1. 2. 3. 4.	1. 2. 3. 4.
THURSDAY	1. 2. 3. 4.	1. 2. 3. 4.	1. 2. 3. 4.
FRIDAY	1. 2. 3. 4.	1. 2. 3. 4.	1. 2. 3. 4.

INFORMATION CODE DIRECTIONS

1. Number of times you forgot = ___ (T = times)
2. Signs to show types of feelings each day:

   ☺ Good   ☐ Okay   ◩ Bad   ■ Very Bad

3. If you decided to quit doing the exercise:

   ✔ = Yes   X = NO
4. Add any other information you wish.

5–10

DANGEROUS HEALTH HABITS

Objective

To have the children explore the difficulty of breaking unhealthy habits, and to become aware of the need to make choices in the future to maintain good health.

Purpose

To improve coping skills.
To clarify personal values and attitudes.

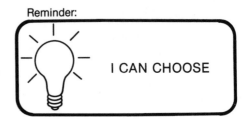

Reminder:

I CAN CHOOSE

Activities

1. Explore the following questions with the children after reviewing activity 5–9, "Breaking Habits."

   a. Is it hard to break a habit?

   b. If a habit is dangerous for your health, is it important to stop it?

   c. Have the children talk to people who smoke cigarettes. Assign the "Cigarette Smoking Questionnaire" (5–10A) for homework.

   d. After the assignment has been completed, discuss the information in the questionnaire. Ask: Did the smokers know it was unhealthy to smoke? Does it make it easier to stop a bad habit if you know it is dangerous to your health? (Unfortunately, it is not any easier.)

2. Discuss the fact that many drugs can be habit-forming. Ask: Is it better or easier not to develop a bad habit, than it is to break the habit? Is thinking about the consequences of our actions before we do something important? Are the risks worth the possible dangers and pain?

3. Do we have choices? Changing unhealthy habits is difficult. To demonstrate: Ask for two right-handed children to volunteer to use only their left hands to write, eat, and so forth, for the rest of the day. Ask them to share some of their feelings and ideas with the class at the end of the day.

> *Note: Identify these experiences as a small discomfort compared to the extreme effort that is required to stop smoking, drinking alcohol, or taking drugs when they become habits. These things can become even stronger than a bad habit. It could become an addiction, which may require help to stop.*

Name _____

Date _____

Cigarette Smoking
Questionnaire

Person	Age	How Many Years Smoking?	Tried to Quit? Yes No	How Many Times?	Do You Know It Is Bad for Your Health? Yes No
1.					
2.					
3.					
4.					
5.					

CIGARETTE SMOKING IS HAZARDOUS TO YOUR HEALTH

5–11

"SMOKING IS DANGEROUS TO YOUR HEALTH"

Objective

To have the children focus on cigarette smoking as the cause of serious health problems.

Purpose

To improve decision-making skills.
To improve coping skills.

Activities

Note: Evidence continued to mount relating the effects of cigarette smoking to serious health problems. Warning the public could no longer be avoided. As of November, 1970, cigarette packages had to carry labels warning of cigarette smoking's danger. The first label read: "Warning: The Surgeon General Has Determined That Cigarette Smoking Is Dangerous to Your Health." See activity 6–7, "The Dangers of Smoking," for the new Surgeon General's Warning Labels (activity sheet 6–7A).

---

1. Review the Cigarette Smoking Fact Sheet given in Appendix 2A.

2. Use the picture on the "Effects of Cigarette Smoking on a Person" activity sheet (5–11A) to identify and study the effects of cigarette smoking on a person.

3. As a homework assignment, to further reinforce the information learned about the effects of cigarette smoking on the body, direct the children to put an "X" in the circle of *five* parts of a person affected by cigarette smoking, as shown in the "Getting the Picture" activity sheet (5–11B). Have them name the areas. In class, discuss the area circled, and what effect cigarette smoking had on that area.

4. Discuss ways of saying "no" without feeling weak or uncomfortable:

   Examples:

   "No, it makes my teeth feel dirty."
   "No, I just brushed my teeth."

"No, I want to play soccer (or other sport), and it may slow me down."

"No, I don't want to spend money on cigarettes, I'm saving for a _____."

"No, I have to get back to _____ now. See you later."

"No, I don't like the way it tastes."

"No, I don't want to!"

The children may continue to contribute "no" sentences to practice and be prepared to say "no" for themselves.

Reminder:

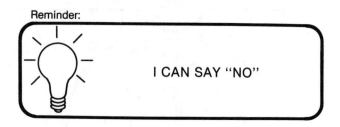

I CAN SAY "NO"

Name _____

Date _____

Effects of Cigarette Smoking on a Person

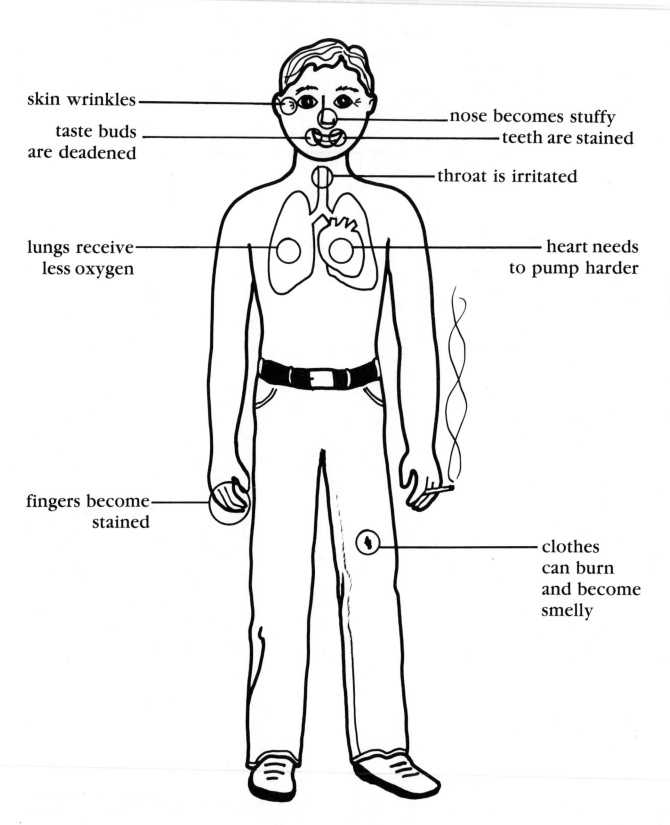

skin wrinkles

taste buds
are deadened

lungs receive
less oxygen

fingers become
stained

nose becomes stuffy

teeth are stained

throat is irritated

heart needs
to pump harder

clothes
can burn
and become
smelly

Name _____

Date _____

Getting the Picture

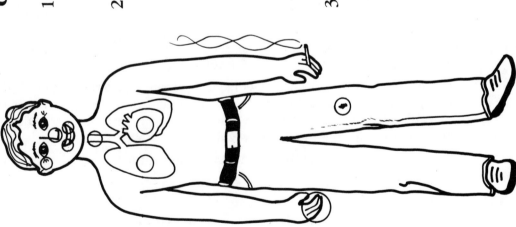

1. Identify five areas affected by cigarette smoking by putting an "X" in the circles on the figure on this page.

2. Name the areas marked with the "X." Write one word that will tell something cigarette smoking does to that area.

   (a) _____

   (b) _____

   (c) _____

   (d) _____

   (e) _____

3. Write two sentences that will help you practice saying "no" to cigarette smoking:

   (a) "No, _____ ."

   (b) "No, _____ ."

CIGARETTE SMOKING
IS A DANGEROUS HEALTH HABIT.

5–12

ATTITUDES ABOUT ALCOHOL

Objective

To have the children identify some personal and societal attitudes about alcohol.

Purpose

To improve decision-making skills.
To clarify personal attitudes and values.

Activities

1. Have the children define the word "attitude" (a manner of *acting, thinking,* or *feeling* that shows one's position or opinion).

2. Discuss some of the ways the students think they may have learned about alcohol use. Which person or situation was the greatest influence? Why?

3. Have the students write the first five words that come to their minds when they hear the word "alcohol."

   a. Discuss why they relate these words to "alcohol." What attitude does it suggest? Was it scared, funny, embarrassed, angry, sad, or confused?

   b. Have the students ask five adults, "What is the first word that comes into your mind when I say 'alcohol'?" Does their reply tell you anything about their attitude?

4. To prepare for a discussion with the class about the attitudes that television commercials or magazine advertisements give the viewer about the use of alcohol (makes one look macho, sophisticated, powerful), have the children review for homework two television commercials or two magazine advertisements. Talk about how they may influence our attitudes.

5. Direct the children to make a collage of alcohol advertisements. Make one that *promotes* the use of alcohol. Make one that *shows the dangers* of alcohol (fighting, drunk driving, etc.). What attitudes do they express? Discuss and evaluate the information in both collages.

6. Ask: Will new information about alcohol and other drugs change your attitude? Why? Discuss.

Reminder:

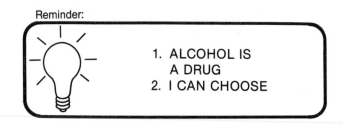

1. ALCOHOL IS A DRUG
2. I CAN CHOOSE

5–13

ALCOHOL AND ITS EFFECTS

Objective

To help the children increase their knowledge about the drug, alcohol, and its effects.

Purpose

To improve decision-making ability.
To clarify personal values and attitudes.

> *Note:* **Emphasize to the children that** alcohol is a drug *that affects the way the body naturally works. Alcohol reaches the brain almost immediately after it is consumed. The brain is the control center of the body. Alcohol is a depressant, sedative drug that slows the body processes. When an adult drinks small amounts of alcohol, the effect is one of relaxation. As the person drinks more, the alcohol begins to have an effect on those parts of the brain that control judgment, coordination, speech, vision, and behavior.*

Activities

1. Have the children define the words:
   (1) slight, (2) moderate, (3) excess.

2. Discuss some ways that alcohol can be used without causing problems:

   a. At rituals—name some religions that use wine in their worship services.

   b. For cooking to add flavor—have the students ever observed wine being used in their homes to make sauces or gravies? Liquor also can enrich the taste of fruit desserts. Have them ask their parents for a recipe in which wine is used.

   c. For medicinal use—occasionally, a glass of sherry might be ordered by a physician for an elderly person to take before bedtime.

   d. For celebration—have the children share stories of wine or champagne being served to give "toasts," at celebrations they may have attended. (When alcoholic beverages are used by adults in moderation, on occasion, in social situations, it is likely that no problems will develop.)

> *Note:* **Support the fact that** abstinence *is an acceptable choice. One can,* ***without need to explain,*** *choose not to drink.*

3. Talk with the children about situations in which alcoholic beverages can be *misused:*

   a. To show one is part of a group, or that one is "cool" or grown-up.

   b. To help deal with, or run away from, life's problems.

   c. Before legal age.

   d. To make oneself "feel better" when one is experiencing uncomfortable feelings of anger, jealousy, hurt, embarrassment, fear, hate, and so on, instead of using other *coping skills.* These behaviors may lead to *abuse* of alcohol.

4. Have each student ask at least two adults about their views on drinking alcohol. They may then give reports to the class for discussion.

Reminder:

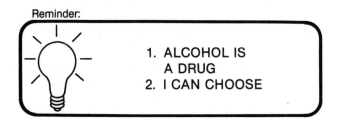

1. ALCOHOL IS A DRUG
2. I CAN CHOOSE

5–14

EFFECTS OF "TOO MUCH" ALCOHOL

Objective

To have the children explore and demonstrate some of the effects of drinking "too much" alcohol.

Purpose

To improve decision-making skills.
To clarify personal values and attitudes.

Activities

1. Explore and demonstrate some physical effects that may be observed when someone has been drinking to excess. Use role-play.

   a. Clear an area for safety; select a student or ask for a student volunteer to spin around for 10 or 15 seconds, until he or she feels dizzy. Ask him or her to:

      (1) walk a straight line.

      (2) write his or her own name.

      (3) pour water from one glass to another.

   b. Check to determine *how long* the student remained feeling dizzy. Ask him or her to try to imagine what would happen if someone felt dizzy for several hours. If someone were ill and needed your help, could you help them?

   c. Role-play a person who is drunk:

      (1) cooking a meal in his or her own house.

      (2) in a store.

      (3) in a factory with machinery.

      (4) driving a car.

2. Why do you think people sometimes laugh at someone who is drunk? Do drunk people look funny? Could being drunk be dangerous? What are some dangerous things that could happen?

3. Talk about the *disease* of *alcoholism*. (Affirm that not everyone who drinks will have the disease.)

Note: Alcoholism is a disease. *The alcoholic is:*

a. *a sick person.*

b. *in need of help to get better.*

c. *not able to control his or her drinking. The alcoholic cannot decide when to stop once he or she begins drinking. These sick people find themselves drinking more than they had planned.*

d. *faced with many problems in life as the result of excessive use of the depressant drug.*

e. *going to get steadily worse unless he or she gets help to stop drinking (Alcoholics Anonymous or similar treatment).*

The people who care about the alcoholic are affected by the disease also. They also need help to be happy again. Al-Anon and Alateen can help.

4. Explore: How do you think people who drink and get drunk feel the next day, physically and mentally? Could they feel embarrassed or ashamed?

5. Play the game "Getting the Message":

a. Follow the directions given on page 133.

b. Cut out the face game board (5–14A).

c. Paste the questions on cardboard or oaktag after they have been cut into game cards from the activity sheet (5–14B).

Note: The students may continue to add "true" and "false" questions to the game as the term progresses.

Reminder:

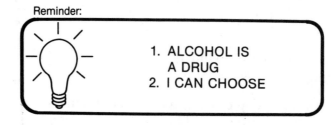

1. ALCOHOL IS
   A DRUG
2. I CAN CHOOSE

Directions for ''Getting the Message'' Game

For: Two or more players.
Use: Pennies or buttons as playing pieces to move on the board and a die.

Directions:

1. Each player will take a turn tossing the die.

2. On his or her turn the player will move the piece on the board the number of spaces showing on the die.

3. The player will do what is appropriate according to the space landed on, as follows:

   a. Where the ''?'' appears, the *other* player will pick a card to read to the player who made the move. (The answer appears on the card.) If the answer is given correctly, the player will *move ahead one space*. If the answer is incorrect, the player who is making the move will *go back two* spaces.

   b. If an ''X'' is landed on, it means, ''You need more information. *Don't make a move and lose one turn.*''

4. The next player takes his or her turn. If the piece lands on the ''?,'' the *other* player reads the question to him or her.

5. The first player to reach ''Finish'' by the gameboard's ear (which signifies their ability to *hear* more *new* information in the future), wins the game.

"Getting the Message" Face Board

Everyone has some weaknesses and some strengths. True	All choices have consequences. True	All problems have solutions. False
No one can make a decision until he is of "legal" age. False	TV advertisers really do not care if you buy their products. They just want to give you information. False	A healthy way of coping with uncomfortable (bad) feelings is to talk with someone you trust about them. True
Using drugs or alcohol is an acceptable way of coping with uncomfortable feelings. False	All habits are bad. False	It is better not to develop an unhealthy habit, because habits are hard to break. True
If you feel irritable when you are trying to break a bad habit, you should stop trying. False	Many drugs are habit-forming and can lead to serious problems when not used properly. True	If one teaspoon of medicine is ordered by the doctor to help you get better, two teaspoons make you better faster. False
You should not take medicines that are outdated. True	We can improve how we do things by comparing ourselves to others. False	Cigarette smoking is an easy habit to stop. False
Everyone has talents. True	Medicines should be kept out of the reach of children. True	Everyone who drinks alcohol will become an alcoholic. False
Caffeine, which can be found in coffee, tea, chocolate, and soda, is a drug. True	You cannot get to be an alcoholic by drinking only beer. False	Our friends can influence the decisions we make, if we always do things to remain part of the group. True

I don't have to finish taking medicines given by my doctor. When I feel better, I can stop taking it. False	Mary offered me some of her medicine. I know it is okay for me to take it, because we both have a cold. False	I am sad. It's okay to take an extra piece of cake to feel better. False
It's best to throw out the bottle because it has no label on it. True	Drinking too much alcohol affects the way you think and act. True	I can choose not to smoke cigarettes. True
It's okay to share your medicines with someone else. False	Mixing drugs and alcohol can kill you. True	The brain is the area in the body most sensitive to the presence of alcohol. True
The brain is the control center of the body. True	It is better to exercise to relax, than it is to take a pill to relax. True	Alcoholism is a disease that can be treated. True
Abstinence means you have decided not drink. True	Cigarette smoking has been proven to be harmful to your health. True	Families of alcoholics suffer. They need help to feel better, too. True
People who drink should not drive. True	It's important to ask for help if I have a problem I can't handle. True	Drugs affect everyone the same way. False
Alcoholics Anonymous is an organization of alcoholics that gives other alcoholics support to get better. True	Al-Anon is an organization of alcoholics that gives other alcoholics support to get better. False	If there is an accident or poisoning I can call for help. I should give my name, address, and the problem. True

-6-

ACTIVITIES FOR GRADE 5

A. Parent Letter

B. *Activity Titles*

		Objectives
6–1	Change How You Feel	To identify feelings and practice ways of expressing them, and to learn about healthy ways to change the way one feels.
6–2	Working Together	To recognize that we are social beings and to practice ways of relating to others.
6–3	Use Your Imagination	To use one's creativity and imagination to expand perceptions and learn new things about one's self.
6–4	Recognizing a Conflict	To discuss the physical and emotional feelings associated with conflict (tension) and explore ways of dealing with them.
6–5	Dealing with Conflict	To explore ways of dealing with conflict.
6–6	Taking a Stand	To explore how the power of others influences one's attitude and behavior.
6–7	The Dangers of Smoking	To research and study factual information about the dangers of cigarette smoking.
6–8	Advertising and Choices	To become aware of the effects of advertising on the choices one makes.
6–9	Alcohol and Its Effects on the Body's Organs	To identify the physical and behavioral effects produced by alcohol on the brain and other body organs.

Dear Parent,

Activities for the fifth grade students have been prepared based on sound principles of growth and development, to positively influence your child in forming healthy ways to deal with him- or herself and others. Addressing these issues *prior* to the time when alcohol and other drug use are most likely to occur increases the probability that your child will not yield to those pressures that frequently lead to substance abuse. These activities will help your child to

1. Identify feelings and practice ways of expressing them and healthy ways to change the way he or she feels.
2. Use creativity and imagination to expand his or her perceptions and to learn new things about him- or herself.
3. Discuss the physical and emotional feelings associated with conflict (tension) and explore ways of dealing with them.
4. Explore how the power of others influences attitude and behavior.
5. Research and study factual information about the dangers of cigarette smoking.
6. Become aware of the effects of advertising on the choices we make.
7. Identify the physical and behavioral effects of alcohol on the brain and other body organs.

We cannot protect our children from facing many of the problems of growing up in today's society, but we can prepare them for this task. Your interest, support, and caring interaction will assist your child in arriving at healthy attitudes and skills.

_____
Teacher

-6-

ACTIVITIES FOR GRADE 5

A. Parent Letter

B. *Activity Titles*   *Objectives*

6–1	Change How You Feel	To identify feelings and practice ways of expressing them, and to learn about healthy ways to change the way one feels.
6–2	Working Together	To recognize that we are social beings and to practice ways of relating to others.
6–3	Use Your Imagination	To use one's creativity and imagination to expand perceptions and learn new things about one's self.
6–4	Recognizing a Conflict	To discuss the physical and emotional feelings associated with conflict (tension) and explore ways of dealing with them.
6–5	Dealing with Conflict	To explore ways of dealing with conflict.
6–6	Taking a Stand	To explore how the power of others influences one's attitude and behavior.
6–7	The Dangers of Smoking	To research and study factual information about the dangers of cigarette smoking.
6–8	Advertising and Choices	To become aware of the effects of advertising on the choices one makes.
6–9	Alcohol and Its Effects on the Body's Organs	To identify the physical and behavioral effects produced by alcohol on the brain and other body organs.

Dear Parent,

Activities for the fifth grade students have been prepared based on sound principles of growth and development, to positively influence your child in forming healthy ways to deal with him- or herself and others. Addressing these issues *prior* to the time when alcohol and other drug use are most likely to occur increases the probability that your child will not yield to those pressures that frequently lead to substance abuse. These activities will help your child to

1. Identify feelings and practice ways of expressing them and healthy ways to change the way he or she feels.
2. Use creativity and imagination to expand his or her perceptions and to learn new things about him- or herself.
3. Discuss the physical and emotional feelings associated with conflict (tension) and explore ways of dealing with them.
4. Explore how the power of others influences attitude and behavior.
5. Research and study factual information about the dangers of cigarette smoking.
6. Become aware of the effects of advertising on the choices we make.
7. Identify the physical and behavioral effects of alcohol on the brain and other body organs.

We cannot protect our children from facing many of the problems of growing up in today's society, but we can prepare them for this task. Your interest, support, and caring interaction will assist your child in arriving at healthy attitudes and skills.

_____

Teacher

6–1

CHANGE HOW YOU FEEL

Objective

To have the children identify feelings and practice ways of expressing them, and to have them explore healthy alternatives to change the way they feel.

Purpose

To improve coping skills.

Activities

> *Note:* *Explain to the students that feelings are neither right nor wrong; they just* are. *We are responsible for the way we express our feelings.*

1. Ask the children to describe some of the physical feelings they may experience when they feel
   a. happy (full of energy)
   b. sad (tired, quiet, weak)
   c. scared (sweaty, queasy stomach)
   d. mad (tight muscles)

2. Ask the children to complete the "What's Happening?" activity sheets (6–1A). They are to recognize each feeling; think of a situation in which they might feel that way; and list some things they can do to help themselves feel better, or change their mood. (This exercise may be given as a homework assignment to allow sufficient time for reflection.) Then, discuss the completed assignment with the class to share some coping skills.

3. Have the children complete the "Letting Off Steam" activity sheet (6–1B).
   a. Ask the children to identify the similarities in the pictures.
   b. Talk about "pressure buildup."
   c. How is "pressure buildup" handled in each picture?
   d. What would happen if the "pressure buildup" energy was kept inside?
   e. Talk about safe releases for that energy (letting off steam).

4. Write a list of feelings on the blackboard.

   a. Have a student choose a feeling and role-play it for the class. Allow a minute or two to complete each performance.

   b. After each emotion is acted out, ask the class to *describe* the facial expression, the body posture, the voice (tone and inflection), and the ideas expressed.

   c. To complete the exercise, give the "actors" a task to do while they are *still role-playing the emotion.* Ask: Does how you *feel* affect the way you *behave?* Tasks: eating lunch, taking a test, cleaning your room.

   d. Ask the class to offer suggestions on how to change one's feelings. Examples: exercise, talk, play, relax, replace negative thoughts with positive thoughts.

5. Emotions (feelings) influence how we hear messages. To illustrate, use one sentence: "I need help." Ask volunteers to respond to that simple statement as though they heard it when they were

   a. Happy (One might hear it then, as an *opportunity* to help someone else feel better.)

   b. Sad (One might hear it then, as an *indictment* of one's "inadequacy.")

   c. Mad (One might hear it then, as an *imposition.*)

Reminder:

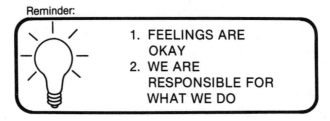

1. FEELINGS ARE OKAY
2. WE ARE RESPONSIBLE FOR WHAT WE DO

What's Happening?

SAD (What)
Situation: (When) Dealing with it: (How)
REJECTED (What)
Situation: (When) Dealing with it: (How)
BORED (What)
Situation: (When) Dealing with it: (How)
HURT (What)
Situation: (When) Dealing with it: (How)
DISAPPOINTED (What)
Situation: (When) Dealing with it: (How)

What's Happening? (continued)

JEALOUS (What)
Situation: (When)
Dealing with it: (How)
ANGRY (What)
Situation: (When)
Dealing with it: (How)
CONFUSED (What)
Situation: (When)
Dealing with it: (How)
SCARED (What)
Situation: (When)
Dealing with it: (How)
LONELY (What)
Situation: (When)
Dealing with it: (How)

Name _____

Date _____

Letting Off Steam

Compare the following pictures. Then, on the back of this sheet, list three *safe* ways you can let off steam.

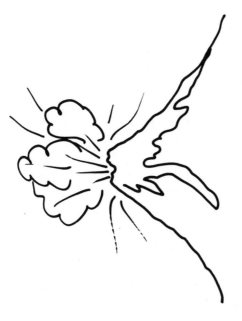

An Erupting Volcano

A Whistling Teakettle

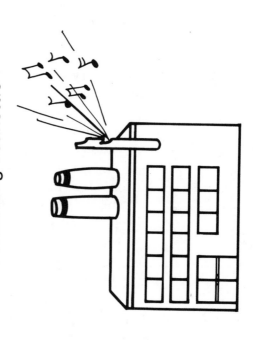

A Person Letting Off Steam

A Factory Whistle

6–2

WORKING TOGETHER

Objective

To teach children to recognize that they are social beings, and to practice ways of relating to others to foster a sense of community and caring.

Purpose

To promote positive self-image.
To improve coping skills.

Activities

1. A joint project may be undertaken at the beginning of the school term. Its purpose is to assist the children in learning more about each individual, while developing a sense of "community." Some suggestions are:

   a. Create a group poster or mural about:

      (1) The history of the town or school, using old snapshots, old newspaper articles, obsolete town maps, and researched stories about these places.

      (2) Foreign countries or U.S. states that class members may have visited using stories and pictures. Have the children form groups to research facts about each country or state. Collect postcards, pictures, and recipes to include in the mural.

      (3) The history of the students' lives. A class "growth project" may be undertaken. It may include:

         (a) *Then:* (1) Have each child bring in a baby picture. (2) Have a contest to determine which student can identify the most baby pictures accurately.

         (b) *Now:* (1) Have each child bring in current pictures showing them involved in some activity or celebration. (2) Allow time to discuss the activities in the pictures.

         (c) *When:* (1) Have each child decide a future goal. Have the children bring in pictures from magazines, brochures, and newspapers that deal with their future goal. (2) Allow time to discuss the reasons for their choice of future goals, as well as the preparation necessary to achieve it.

2. As a group, have the class design holiday cards to send to senior citizens in nursing homes. (The children can become aware of their power to influence others, and feel good about themselves.)

3. For this activity, you may select a partner for each child. This is a good opportunity to encourage *new* combinations in student relationships. Describe and implement the "Blind Trust Walk":

   a. Ask the partners to face each other and hold hands.

   b. Cover the eyes of one of the partners with a blindfold.

   c. Direct the leader, who has his or her eyes *uncovered*, to lead the partner *safely* around the classroom. Each student will take the opportunity to follow and to lead.

   d. Discuss the feelings of being in the position of leader and follower.

Reminder:

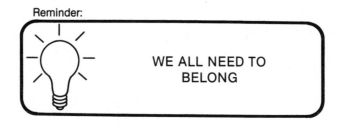

WE ALL NEED TO
BELONG

6–3

USE YOUR IMAGINATION

Objective

To have the children learn new things about themselves and use their creativity and imagination to expand their *perceptions.*

Purpose

To improve self-image.
To improve coping skills.

Activities

> *Note: Emphasize to students that* drugs alter moods. *They do not change a situation or solve a problem, but merely* change *our* perception *of the situation, or of ourselves.*

1. Ask each student to write a short story using the following as topics:
   a. An animal I would like to be. Why?
   b. A flower that I would like to be. Why?
   c. A musical instrument that I would like to be. Why?

2. Have each student invent an imaginary creature. (Encourage creativity.)
   a. Give the creature a name, a place of origin, and a purpose.
   b. What does it eat? Where does it sleep?
   c. Is it friendly?
   d. Make it visual for the class by drawing a picture or creating a puppet.
   e. Make a vocabulary for the creature for basic words of communication: Hello, goodbye, thank you, please.
   f. Describe some of your creature's characteristics that you like and some that you don't like.

3. Ask a student to stand any place in the classroom. Have the student describe what he or she can see without moving his or her head around. Now ask the student to lie on the floor. Tell him or her to look straight ahead again, without moving his or her head around. Ask the student to describe what he or she can see. (Emphasize that only his or her *view* has changed. All things in the room remain the same.)

4. Instruct the students to:

   a. Trace each other's body shape onto paper from a large roll, to make a complete body form.

   b. Cut out pictures or use materials that tell something about themselves. Indicate what he or she likes and doesn't like relating to foods, recreation, clothes, music, animals, friends, etc. Attach or paste the items within the body form. Leave some empty spaces for classmates to "complete the picture."

   c. Have them outline the pictures that show things they do not like in red and outline pictures of things they like in blue.

   d. After the exercise has been completed, stand back to get an overview of the body form. What color appeared most often?

   e. Request five classmates to "complete the picture" by adding pictures or words that they feel describe their classmate. (Remind the students to be tactful.)

5. Ask the students to write autobiographies which will be collected.

   a. Ask them not to put their names on them.

   b. You can put a number on each paper and put the number for each autobiography on individual pieces of paper, fold them up, and put them in a box.

   c. Have a student pick a number out of the box and read aloud the corresponding autobiography.

   d. Can the class guess who it is?

Reminder:

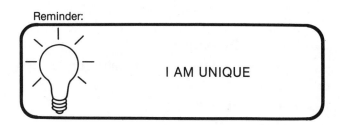

I AM UNIQUE

6–4

RECOGNIZING A CONFLICT

Objective

To encourage the children to discuss the physical and emotional feelings associated with conflict (tension).

Purpose

To explore decision-making skills.
To improve coping skills.
To clarify values.

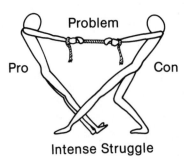

Activities

Have the children:

1. Define the word "conflict." (Being pulled in two directions as in a tug of war; a struggle.)

2. Describe some of the physical symptoms from the struggle (tight muscles, headache, restlessness, for example).

3. Describe some emotional symptoms (irritability, distraction, preoccupation, short temper).

4. Give some examples of conflicts:

   study ←→ play   eat ←→ diet

   hoard ←→ share   face it ←→ avoid it

5. Create stories with "conflicts" in them. Use puppets to act out conflicting goals and ideas.

6. Define some conflicts in books you have read (including fairy tales). How were some of the conflicts resolved?

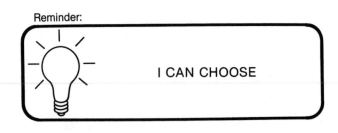

6–5

DEALING WITH CONFLICT

Objective

To have the children explore new ways of dealing with conflicts.

Purpose

To improve decision-making skills.
To improve coping skills.
To clarify personal values.

Activities

1. Have the class choose an issue that might create a conflict. Explore methods of dealing with it. Use the following steps to help in making a decision:

   Example:

   a. Identify the conflict. (Should I _____ or _____?)

   b. Explore the choices and the consequences.
      (1) Divide a piece of paper in half.
      (2) On one side write a list of the positive possibilities (pros).
      (3) On the other side write a list of the negative possibilities (cons).
      (4) Use a number evaluation from 1 (the lowest rating) to 10 (the highest rating) to see how the sides "add up." (See Figure 6–1.)

   c. Are you willing to "pay the price?" Do you understand the trade-offs" (the consequences)?

   d. Make a *decision.* (All decisions are subject to change if they prove ineffective over a period of time.)

2. Have two students role-play each part of a conflict going on inside a person. One will take the positive possibilities; the other will show the negative possibilities.

FIGURE 6–1.

PROBLEM: Should I smoke cigarettes?

1. 1–10 Number Evaluation	Pros	1–10 Number Evaluation	Cons
	It shows I'm grown up.		I could develop health problems.
	All my friends smoke and I want to be part of the group.		Shortness of breath may interfere with sports.
	It peps me up.		It costs a lot of money.
	It helps me when I feel nervous.		My family will be upset.
_____ TOTAL		TOTAL _____	

Note: Encourage the students to focus on the *healthy alternatives* to the conflict:

Save the money to buy a bike.

Work out to stay fit so one can *join a team* and *become part of a group.*

Practice thinking for oneself, and *choose not to smoke* even though some friends smoke, because it is a proven health hazard.

Learn other ways of handling being "nervous" such as jogging, talking to a friend, starting a hobby that takes attention away from worries, practicing deep breathing, and so forth.

3. DECISION: _____ ? _____   4. ACCEPT THE CONSEQUENCES!

I CAN CHOOSE!

Example:

BOTH SIDES OF THE STORY

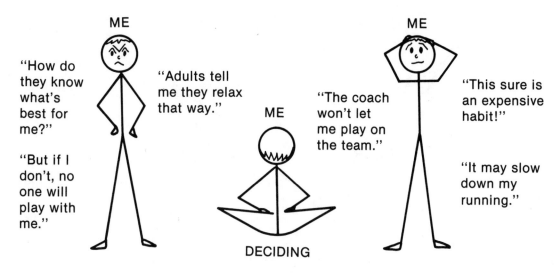

3. Ask the children:
   a. Do you think you will be pressured to smoke, drink, or use drugs?
   b. Will you have conflicts (a tug of war inside of you due to peer pressure, media pressure, and so forth)?
   c. Will you review the consequences before you make a decision?
4. Complete the "A Conflict in My Life" activity sheet (6–5A).

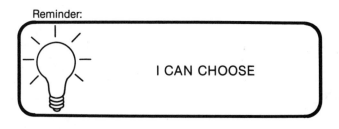

A Conflict in My Life

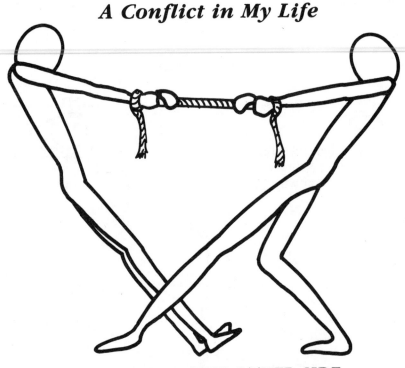

MY SIDE VS. THE OTHER SIDE

Select a situation in your life that occurred recently with your parents, brothers or sisters, or classmates or friends. Present the information in the form of newspaper headlines, which will make the problem and your solution clear to the reader.

HEADLINES

1. The Problem   _____

2. My Side   _____

3. The Other Side   _____

4. Some Solutions   _____

                         _____

                         _____

                         _____

                         _____

5. My Decision   _____
6. How I Feel Now,
   Looking Back   _____

7. What I Have Learned   _____

6–6

TAKING A STAND

Objective

To have the children explore the powers of others in influencing one's attitudes and behavior.

Purpose

To improve decision-making ability.
To clarify attitudes and values.
To develop social responsibilities.

Activities

1. Ask the students to *spontaneously* answer the "what if" questions that follow. After they have used that approach, have the class explore the questions more completely, following the recommended steps for problem solving: (1) *defining* the problem; (2) *collecting* information to explore solutions/alternatives; (3) *examining* the consequences for each solution.
   What would you do if . . .

   a. Someone challenged you to a fight after school? Why?

   b. Everyone was going to come in late to school one morning to protest the suspension of a student? Why?

   c. Someone challenged you to smoke a cigarette? Why?

   d. Someone challenged you to drink a can of beer? Why?

   e. You were the only one in the class not invited to a party? Why?

2. Ask the students to role-play the following:

   a. You are the one *being pressured* by the group to do something you really are not sure you want to do. How does it feel emotionally? (Act afraid, angry, sad, confused.) How does it feel physically? (Do you perspire, have tight muscles, will your heart beat faster, will you blush?)

   b. You are the one in the group *exerting pressure* on a person to do something he or she may not want to do. How do you feel about being part of the group? How do you feel about the person being pressured? Would you feel responsible if he or she were hurt in any way when he or she accepted your challenge? Why?

3. How often do you think you do things just because your friends are doing them?

4. Discuss whether the students feel they make most of their own decisions. Ask them to give some examples.

5. Play the game of "Simple Simon" with the students.

   a. Each may have an opportunity to be the leader. Discuss how it feels to be a leader.

   b. Ask: How did it feel to be a follower? Were you comfortable in both roles? Were you more comfortable in one of the roles? Which one?

6. Talk about role models. Ask: Who is the person you would *most* want to be like? Why? Name a person from each category in the following list that you admire. Write a profile about that person. What do you most admire about him or her?

   a. an actor or actress

   b. an athlete

   c. a TV character

   d. an older friend or sibling

   e. a parent

   f. a political or religious figure

7. Research a story of a person who "went against the tide" and followed what he or she believed, even though the majority disagreed.

Reminder:

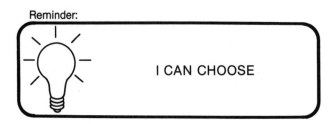

6–7

THE DANGERS OF SMOKING

Objective

To have the children research and study factual information about the dangers of cigarette smoking.

Purpose

To improve decision-making skills.
To clarify personal attitudes and values.

Activities

1. Study and discuss the *fact sheets* on the dangers of cigarette smoking as shown in Appendix 2A.

2. Define and report on words that are related to cigarette smoking:

addictive	depressant	tars
bronchi	nicotine	tolerance
carbon monoxide	pollution	peer pressure
dependent fetus	respiratory	withdrawal

3. Have the children discuss the Surgeon General's four warnings as shown on the activity sheet (6–7A).

4. Have the children ask the adults they know *why* they smoke. Explore with the class other *alternatives* that can be used to satisfy these reasons. Complete the "A Hot Issue" activity sheet (6–7B).

5. Ask the students to respond to the following statements. They are to use facts that they know about cigarette smoking in their answers:

   a. "I feel fine now even though I smoke."

   b. "It's such a strong habit. I *can't* change it. I've tried."

   c. "The damage is already done."

   d. "I'm only hurting myself."

   e. "All my friends smoke."

6. Contact the local American Cancer Society or American Lung Association to have a speaker come in to give a talk or to receive materials to use for teaching about the dangers of cigarette smoking.

7. Have the children check the newspapers, over a period of a week or more, for stories of fires which may have been caused by careless cigarette smoking, and report on this to the class.

8. Have the children observe and report on places where they notice separate sections for smokers and nonsmokers (theater, restaurants, airplanes, waiting rooms, and so on).

9. Review activities 5–8, 5–9, and 5–10, which deal with habits. (The information and exercises remain pertinent to all K–6 grade students.)

10. Design a poster or bumper sticker for an antismoking campaign.

11. Ask the children to complete the "Going Up in Smoke" crossword puzzle (6–7C).

12. Complete the "Cigarette Smoking Worksheet" (6–7D). The worksheet's answers are:

1. T	7. T
2. F	8. T
3. T	9. F
4. F	10. T
5. T	11. T
6. F	12. T

Reminder:

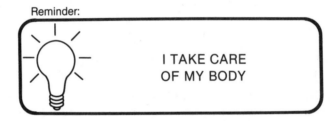

I TAKE CARE
OF MY BODY

Date _____

The Surgeon General's Warnings

WARNING: The Surgeon General has determined that smoking is hazardous to your health.

As of October 1985, new warnings are being issued by the Surgeon General. There are to be *four* warnings which will be rotated every three months.

1. "Smoking causes lung cancer, heart disease, emphysema, and may complicate pregnancy."

2. "Quitting smoking now greatly reduces serious risks to your health."

3. "Smoking by pregnant women may result in fetal injury, premature birth, and low birth weight."

4. "Cigarette smoke contains carbon monoxide."

A Hot Issue

List five "reasons" that people say they smoke.

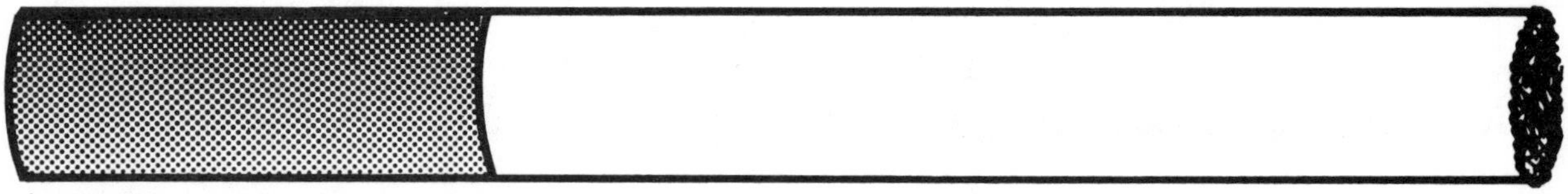

1.

2.

3.

4.

5.

List five alternative ways these people could meet their needs—without smoking.

1. _____

2. _____

3. _____

4. _____

5. _____

Name _____   6–7C

Date _____

Going Up in Smoke

ACROSS

2. The Surgeon General says there are no _____ cigarettes.

3. A waste product of cigarette smoking is _____. (2 words)

5. Cigarette smoking can lead to _____ disease.

6. Cigarette smoking is the major single cause of _____ cancer.

8. Cigarette smoking stains a person's _____.

9. The cancer-causing substances in cigarettes are called _____.

10. Young people (10–18 years of age) smoke chiefly because of _____ pressure.

DOWN

1. The poison found in cigarettes is called _____.

2. _____ affects nonsmokers in the surrounding area.

4. The chief single avoidable cause of death is _____ smoking.

7. Smoking by pregnant women may hurt the _____.

WORD LIST

carbon monoxide   lung
fetus   safe
peer   teeth
cigarette   nicotine
tars   heart
smoking

Name _____

Date _____

Cigarette Smoking Worksheet

List five "reasons" people give for *not* smoking.

_____

_____

_____

_____

_____

Answer the following questions, true or false:

1. The tars in cigarettes are cancer-causing agents. _____

2. It is safe to smoke filtered cigarettes. _____

3. Nicotine is a poison found in tobacco. _____

4. Quitting smoking will not improve your health. _____

5. Cigarette smoking can lead to heart disease. _____

6. Smoke from cigarette harms only the smoker. _____

7. Peer pressure is the reason many young people between the ages of 10 and 18 begin experimenting with smoking. _____

8. Cigarette smoking is the major single cause of cancer in the United States. _____

9. Only the lungs are affected by smoking cigarettes. _____

10. The Surgeon General has said that packages of cigarettes must show health warnings to tell people of the dangers of cigarette smoking. _____

11. I can get more information about the dangers of smoking from the American Lung Association. _____

12. I can choose not to smoke. _____

6–8

ADVERTISING AND CHOICES

Objective

To have the students become more aware of the effects of advertising on the choices they make.

Purpose

To improve decision-making skills.
To explore personal attitudes and values.

Activities

1. Have the children collect alcohol and cigarette advertisements from as many different types of magazines and periodicals as possible (sports, glamour, ethnic, etc.). Discuss how these ads try to appeal to their clientele.

2. List other ways of meeting the needs to which these ads are appealing (beauty, power, belonging to the "in" crowd, maturity, sophistication, relaxation).

3. Ask each student to design an ad for a product. Pick a particular group to influence. Have the class discuss what influence it has on them. Why? Can they pick out what message is conveyed?

4. Have the students design an alcohol advertisement *for* drinking, and *against* drinking.

5. Design a cigarette ad for a magazine.

6. Present the completed ads to the class for review.

7. Discuss a television advertisement that appeals to them. Why?

8. Role-play some television advertisements omitting the names of the products. Can the class guess which product is being advertised? Why did the child choose this particular advertisement?

9. Ask: Will alcohol advertisements have any effect upon your decision to use alcohol in the future? Do you feel pressure? Make a list of words in the ads that make you feel that it is "good" to drink alcohol. Discuss.

Reminder:

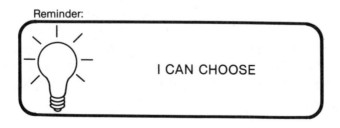

I CAN CHOOSE

6–9

ALCOHOL AND ITS EFFECTS
ON THE BODY'S ORGANS

Objective

To have the children learn about the drug, alcohol. They will identify the physical and behavioral effects produced by alcohol on the brain and the other body organs.

Purpose

To improve decision-making ability.
To clarify attitudes and values.

Activities

1. Study all of the activity sheets for "The Effects of Alcohol on the Body's Organs" (6–9A through 6–9F). (All of the sheets can be duplicated for the children to keep.)

2. Have the children find the definition of the following words in the dictionary:

drug	tolerance	ingestion
intoxication	prohibition	digestion
detoxification	dependency	absorption
abstinence	moderation	alcoholism

3. Have the students write a research paper on an alcohol-related topic.

   Examples:

   a. The history of alcohol in the United States
   b. Different cultural attitudes toward drinking
   c. The period of Prohibition in the United States
   d. The use of alcohol (wine) in religious services

4. Review newspaper articles to see how many of the stories that relate to violence (fights, fires, car accidents, etc.) involve the use of alcohol. Report on this to the class. (You can encourage the students to talk about alcohol's effect on the area of the brain which regulates inhibitions, judgment, and self-control, as shown on "The Brain" activity sheet (6–9D). Stress that people will do things that they could not ordinarily do when under the influence of alcohol.)

5. Clear an area in the classroom to ensure safety. Place a strip of masking tape in a straight line on the floor.

   a. Ask for a volunteer to spin around for 15 to 20 seconds. Then ask the student to

      (1) pour water from one glass into another glass

      (2) write his or her name

      (3) walk a straight line (using the masking tape as a guide)

   b. How well did the volunteer perform these activities?

   c. How long did the dizziness last? What would it be like if it lasted for hours, as though it was from drug intoxication?

6. Clear an area for safety and ask for another volunteer who will spin around for 15 to 20 seconds to get dizzy. Have the other students in the class set a scene to which the volunteer will respond immediately, i.e.:

   "You are crossing a busy street. There is a car coming rapidly from the right side. . . ."

   "Your house is on fire; you have two minutes to take what you value out of the house. . . ."

7. Complete the "How to Tell Your Blood-Alcohol Level" activity sheet (6–9E). Does alcohol affect everyone in the same way?

8. Have several students role-play a scene of a group daring someone to drink alcohol. Ask the rest of the class to enter into the role-playing by expressing out loud: (1) some thoughts the one being pressured might be having; (2) what some of the consequences could be of accepting the dare.

9. Have the children read and complete the "Fact or Fiction, Be a 'Know-It-All' " activity sheet (6–9F).

Reminder:

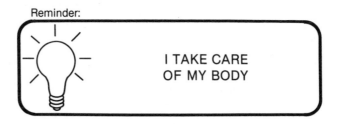

I TAKE CARE
OF MY BODY

Name _____

Date _____

THE EFFECTS OF ALCOHOL
ON BODY ORGANS

GOAL: To Identify the Physical Effects
of Alcohol

PURPOSE: To Increase Knowledge
To Assist in Decision Making

Effects of Alcohol on the Stomach

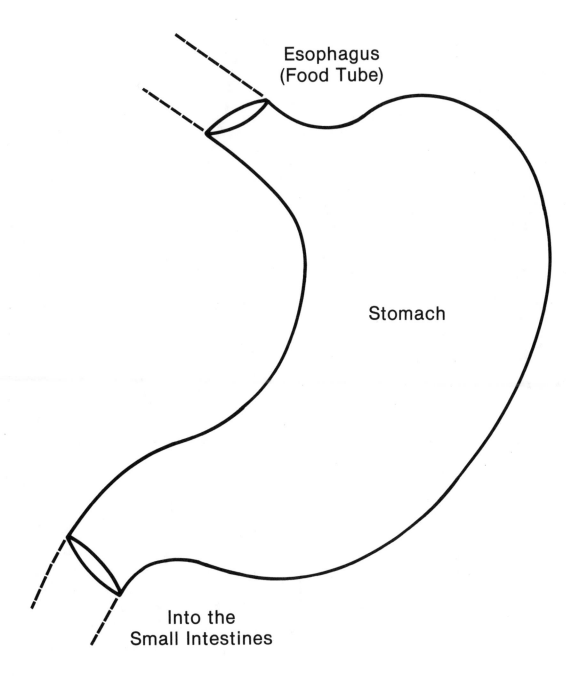

Esophagus
(Food Tube)

Stomach

Into the
Small Intestines

Alcohol has *no* food value. Alcohol is *not digested* in the stomach. Some of the alcohol is absorbed *directly* into the bloodstream through the capillaries (smallest blood vessels). The rest of the alcohol passes into the small intestines where it is absorbed *rapidly* and *completely* into the bloodstream. Alcohol irritates the stomach lining.

The Liver—
The Body's Chemical Factory

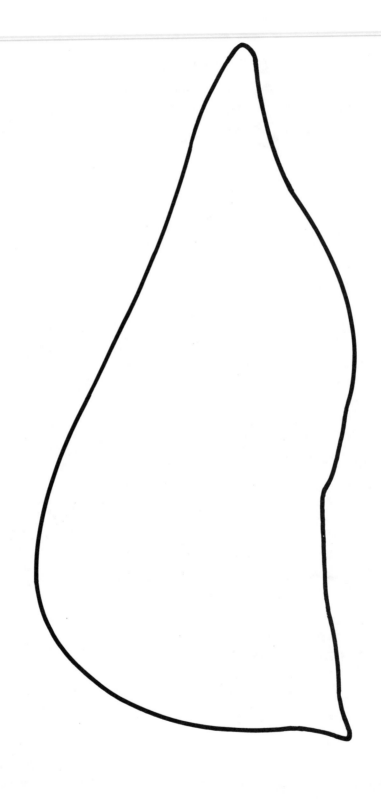

1. The liver aids in digestion.

2. It acts as a *cleansing station* to *rid* the body of *poisons*.

3. The excess use of alcohol can damage the liver and lead to liver disease (cirrhosis).

The Heart

Alcohol causes the heart to lose its normal heartbeat rhythm.
It weakens the strength of the heart muscle contractions.
It may also cause the heart to enlarge or cause heart failure in an advanced stage of alcoholism.

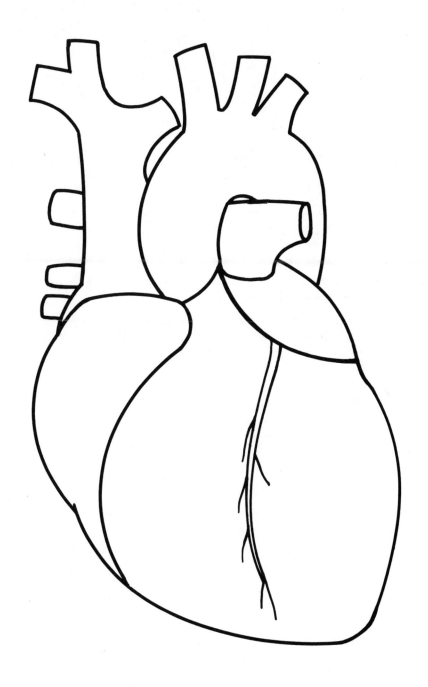

The Brain—The Control Center of the Body

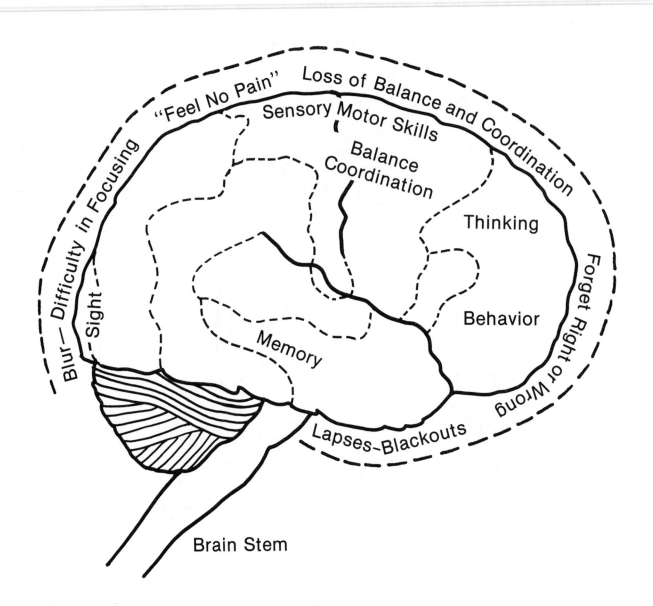

- - - = alcohol affected

The brain is the organ most sensitive to alcohol.

How to Tell Your Blood–Alcohol Level

	120 lb.	140 lb.	160 lb.	180 lb.	200 lb.	220 lb.
12 Drinks	.37	.32	.28	.25	.22	.20
11 Drinks	.34	.29	.25	.22	.20	.18
10 Drinks	.31	.26	.23	.20	.18	.17
9 Drinks	.28	.24	.21	.18	.16	.15
8 Drinks	.25	.21	.18	.16	.15	.13
7 Drinks	.21	.18	.16	.14	.13	.11
6 Drinks	.18	.16	.14	.12	.11	.10
5 Drinks	.15	.13	.11	.10	.09	.08
4 Drinks	.12	.10	.09	.08	.07	.06
3 Drinks	.09	.08	.07	.06	.05	.05
2 Drinks	.06	.05	.04	.04	.03	.03
1 Drink	.03	.02	.02	.02	.01	.01

(Medical Society of New Jersey)

BLOOD-ALCOHOL LEVEL

% of Blood-Alcohol	Intoxicated?	If You Drive
.00 - .04	You have been drinking	Take it easy
.05 - .09	You may be drunk	Use extreme caution
.10 - .14	You are drunk	Let someone else drive
.15 & .up	You are dead drunk	Don't drive!

1 drink = 1 oz. 100% liquor **or** 12 oz. beer **or** 4 oz. table wine

(Medical Society of New Jersey — one hour period)

Color all areas .00–.04 (You have been drinking)   Green
Color all areas .05–.09 (You may be drunk)   Blue
Color all areas above .10 (Legally drunk)   Red
Does alcohol have the *same* effect on everyone?

Be a "Know-It-All"

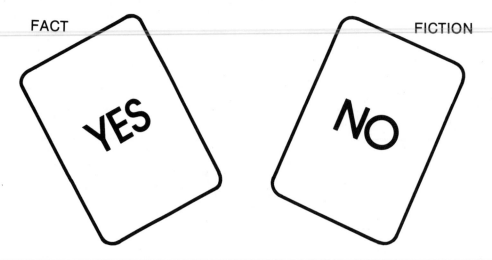

FACT   FICTION

Materials

red construction paper
green construction paper
pair of scissors
black marker

Directions to the Teacher

1. Cut 5 × 8 cards out of both red and green construction paper. Give one green and one red card to each student.

2. On the green card, have the students print "YES" in large letters with the marker. On the red card, print "NO" in large letters with the marker.

3. Each student should have a piece of note paper and a pencil on his or her desk to keep track of the number of questions each answers incorrectly, so the student may do further research or correct his or her errors.

4. You will read the following "Fact or Fiction" questions to the class. All the students will *immediately* respond with the green or red flash card that they think is the correct response. The correct answer will then be given by you. Students will keep their own scores.

5. A secretary may be chosen to keep track of the number of incorrect answers given by the class for each of the questions, in order to determine what information needs further research or study.

6. Leave time after the exercise has been completed for further questions from the children.

7. Leave the "Fact or Fiction" questions in an accessible place for the children to look over at their convenience.

Variation

1. Form two teams with an equal number of students on each side. Have them form lines on each side of the room.

2. Place two bells on each side of your desk at the front of the room.

3. You may stand behind the desk in order to observe which student rings the bell first.

4. You will read the "Fact or Fiction" questions to the class.

5. The lead student on each line will have to ring the bell before he or she answers the question.

6. The student who rings the bell with the correct answer will score one point for the team.

7. The team with the most points wins.

The students may continue to create questions concerning drugs, their use, misuse, and abuse throughout the term. They may add questions dealing with decision-making and coping skills.

FACT OR FICTION

1. Alcohol is a drug.

   (*True*. It is the number-one drug problem in this country.)

2. Drugs are always bad for you.

   (*False*. Drugs can be helpful in times of illness, to prevent disease, to relieve pain, and so forth. It is the misuse of drugs taken for the wrong reasons, in the wrong amount, under the wrong circumstances, that causes problems.)

3. If one teaspoon of medicine is good for you, two teaspoons will make you even better.

   (*False*. The dosage is determined by a person's size, weight, severity of the condition, and other drugs being used. Drugs should be taken only as directed.)

4. Coffee, tea, and cigarettes all contain drugs.

   (*True*. Coffee and tea contain caffeine, which is a stimulant. Cigarettes contain nicotine. See the ''Cigarette Fact Sheet'' in Appendix 2A for more information.)

5. No drug ordered by the doctor can ''hook'' you.

   (*False*. Many drugs ordered by physicians for pain or relief of anxiety can be addictive. It is necessary to take medicines only as directed and for a limited duration of time.)

6. Cigarette smoking can be addictive.

   (*True*. Nicotine is a drug. Like the drug, alcohol, it initially stimulates. Later doses have a depressant effect.)

7. If drugs are in my home, it is okay to use them.

   (*False*. Drugs should not be used by children without the supervision of an adult.)

8. Alcoholics are sick people.

   (*True*. Alcoholism is a disease, just as diabetes or epilepsy is a disease. It responds to treatment.)

9. Drugs can help me to handle my problems better.

   (*False*. The use of drugs helps people forget about their problems for awhile. The problems do not go away. They can get worse.)

10. The disease of alcoholism hurts only the person with the disease.

    (*False*. It hurts their families and the other people who care about the alcoholic. It affects the sick person's job and company that he or she works for. It creates a dangerous situation for other drivers on the highways.)

11. A cup of coffee will help someone who is drunk to sober up.

    (*False*. Only time will cause a person to become sober. It takes one hour for the liver to process one-half ounce of pure alcohol.)

12. Alcohol affects each of us the same way every time we drink.

    (*False.* Factors which influence how alcohol affects the individual include: amount of alcohol taken, the presence of other drugs in the system, the general health of the individual at the time, how recently he or she has eaten, and others. See Appendix 2B–1.)

13. A cold shower helps to sober someone who is drunk.

    (*False.* Only time will help a drunk to become sober.)

14. Being drunk is funny.

    (*False.* It may look funny to others, but it is dangerous. The areas of the brain that control balance, coordination, and good judgment are affected.)

15. You can tell an alcoholic by the way the person looks.

    (*False.* Alcoholism affects people from all walks of life, from all races, from every economic group. Only approximately 3 to 5 percent of alcoholics live on the streets.)

16. Combining drugs without first clearing it with your doctor can be dangerous.

    (*True.* Drugs may have a different effect or more of an effect when used with other drugs. The doctor should know all drugs that you are taking.)

17. When people stop smoking cigarettes they can reverse some of the damage to the body.

    (*True.* If there is no permanent heart or lung damage, the body begins to heal itself when a person stops smoking.)

18. Cigarette smoking will hurt a pregnant woman, but will not hurt her baby.

    (*False.* One of the Surgeon General's Warnings says: "Smoking by pregnant women may result in fetal injury, premature birth, and low birth weight.")

19. Drinking only beer will keep a person from ever having a problem with alcohol.

    (*False.* It is the ethyl alcohol present in the drink that affects each drinker.)

20. The brain is the organ of the body most sensitive to the drug, alcohol. It affects the areas of the brain which control behavior, judgment, sight, speech, and coordination.

    (*True.*)

ACTIVITIES FOR GRADE 6

A. Parent Letter
B. *Activity Titles*   *Objectives*

7–1	Self-Image	To identify personal likes, dislikes, and future goals.
7–2	Roots	To be aware of one's roots and thereby increase one's sense of belonging (security).
7–3	Mood Changes	To explore the effects feelings have on the decisions that we make.
7–4	Choices and Consequences	To recognize the need to make choices and to accept the consequences of these choices.
7–5	Resources for Problem Solving	To identify resources for help in solving problems.
7–6	Brainstorming	To use brainstorming techniques to find solutions for specific problems.
7–7	Cigarette Smoking and Your Body	To identify and discuss some physical effects of cigarette smoking on the body.
7–8	Cigarette Smoking and Societal Attitudes	To identify the present attitudes in society towards smoking.
7–9	Attitudes About Alcohol	To explore personal, family, and community attitudes towards the use of alcohol.
7–10	Alcohol and the Body	To learn about alcohol and improve one's coping and decision-making skills.
7–11	The Blood-Alcohol Concentration Wheel	To learn more about the effects of alcohol on a person by using the BAC Wheel.
7–12	The Disease of Alcoholism	To become more aware of the disease of alcoholism and its effects.
7–13	Positive Peer Pressure	To become aware of one's power to positively influence others.

Dear Parent,

Activities for the sixth grade students have been prepared, based on sound principles of growth and development, to positively influence your child in forming healthy ways to deal with one's self and others. Addressing these issues *prior* to the time when alcohol and other drug use is most likely to occur increases the probability that your child will not yield to those pressures that frequently lead to substance abuse. These activities will help your child to

1. Identify personal likes, dislikes, and future goals.
2. Be aware of his or her roots and increase the student's sense of belonging (security).
3. Explore the effects feelings have on decision making.
4. Recognize the need to make choices and to accept the consequences of those choices.
5. Identify resources for help in solving problems.
6. Use brainstorming techniques to find solutions for specific problems.
7. Identify and discuss some physical effects of cigarette smoking on the body.
8. Identify the present attitudes in society today towards smoking cigarettes.
9. Explore personal, family, and community attitudes towards the use of alcohol.
10. Learn about alcohol and drugs and improve his or her coping and decision-making skills.
11. Become aware of one's power to influence others.

We cannot protect our children from facing many of the problems of growing up in today's society, but we can prepare them for this task. Your interest, support, and caring interaction will assist your child in arriving at healthy attitudes and skills.

_____
Teacher

7–1

SELF-IMAGE

Objective

To have the children recognize that they are unique and worthwhile. They will learn more about themselves by completing the exercises that deal with personal likes, dislikes, characteristics, and future goals.

Purpose

To explore personal values and attitudes.
To improve self-image.

Activities

1. Ask the students to write a biography. They may begin by describing the way they look physically, as though they were writing to someone whom they had never met. Include information about their favorite color, favorite sport, favorite food, favorite TV program, and so forth.

2. Have the children complete the "Self-Discovery" activity sheet (7–1A).

3. Have the children complete the "Preparing for the Journey" activity sheet (7–1B). It may be given as a homework assignment to allow the time necessary for a thoughtful response.

4. Direct the children to complete the "Making News" activity sheet (7–1C). This exercise will encourage them to see the possibilities for their future goals and reinforce the fact that work and preparation are needed to reach these goals.

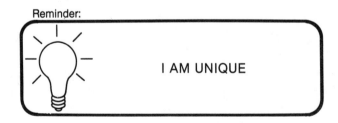

Reminder:

I AM UNIQUE

Self-Discovery

 The one thing that I've done that I am most proud of:

 The dumbest thing I have ever done:

 Three things that scare me:

The place where I feel the happiest is:

 The one trait that I want most people to remember me for:

A future goal I have is: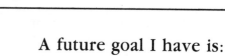

My favorite memory is:

My most annoying habit is:

Preparing for the Journey

Life is like a continuous journey. ''Pack your bags'' for the trip. Circle in *blue* some of the things you want to take with you (keep). Circle in *red* those things you want to improve or change (discard). Circle in *green* those things that you want to work to acquire (get).

crabby	loud	skinny	heavy	petite	gentle
polite	artistic	mature	mean	prudish	slim
outspoken	smart	committed	quiet	thoughtful	unique
attractive	good-natured	two-faced	nervous	lazy	worldly
hard worker	concerned	friendly	stout	vain	spiteful
talented	competitive	moody	cautious	reckless	pretty
shy	studious	poised	fat	well-built	talkative
short	stubborn	tall	angry	rebellious	conceited
spiritual	selfish	dependent	honest	unselfish	clumsy
impatient	sensitive	clever	dedicated	bossy	naive
loyal	athletic	nagging	charming	sad	strong
responsible	direct	accepting	respectful	generous	fearful
creative	forgetful	timid	aggressive	lonely	in a rut
prejudiced	withdrawn	wise	greedy	proud	
energetic	trusting	dishonest	clumsy	peaceful	

Ask a friend or family member to do the exercise to see how they see you.

WE ARE ALL CONTINUOUSLY GROWING AND CHANGING!

© 1986 by Prentice-Hall, Inc.

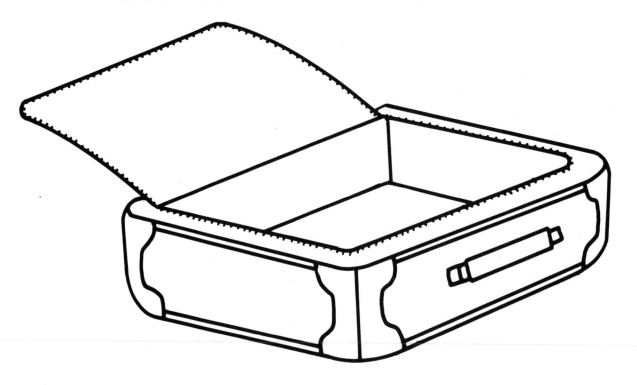

Self-Discovery

 The one thing that I've done that I am most proud of:

 The dumbest thing I have ever done:

 Three things that scare me:

The place where I feel the happiest is: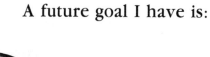

  The one trait that I want most people to remember me for:

A future goal I have is: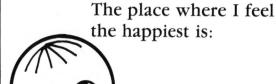

My favorite memory is:

My most annoying habit is:

Preparing for the Journey

Life is like a continuous journey. "Pack your bags" for the trip. Circle in *blue* some of the things you want to take with you (keep). Circle in *red* those things you want to improve or change (discard). Circle in *green* those things that you want to work to acquire (get).

crabby	loud	skinny	heavy	petite	gentle
polite	artistic	mature	mean	prudish	slim
outspoken	smart	committed	quiet	thoughtful	unique
attractive	good-natured	two-faced	nervous	lazy	worldly
hard worker	concerned	friendly	stout	vain	spiteful
talented	competitive	moody	cautious	reckless	pretty
shy	studious	poised	fat	well-built	talkative
short	stubborn	tall	angry	rebellious	conceited
spiritual	selfish	dependent	honest	unselfish	clumsy
impatient	sensitive	clever	dedicated	bossy	naive
loyal	athletic	nagging	charming	sad	strong
responsible	direct	accepting	respectful	generous	fearful
creative	forgetful	timid	aggressive	lonely	in a rut
prejudiced	withdrawn	wise	greedy	proud	
energetic	trusting	dishonest	clumsy	peaceful	

Ask a friend or family member to do the exercise to see how they see you.

WE ARE ALL CONTINUOUSLY GROWING AND CHANGING!

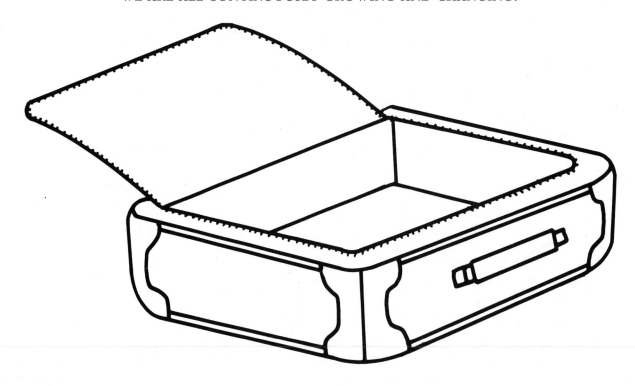

Name _____

Date _____

Making News

```
┌─────────────────────────────────────────────────────────┐
│  ┌──────────────┐  INSIDE      ┌──────────┐  WEATHER     │
│  │              │              │          │              │
│  │              │              │          │  SPORTS      │
│  └──────────────┘              └──────────┘              │
│                                                          │
│              The News                                    │
│                                                          │
│  DATE:                         BY:                       │
│  _____  │
│  _____  │
│  _____  │
│  _____  │
│  _____  │
│  _____  │
│  _____  │
│  _____  │
│  _____  │
│  _____  │
│  _____  │
│  _____  │
│  _____  │
│  _____  │
│  _____  │
│  _____  │
│  _____  │
└─────────────────────────────────────────────────────────┘
```

Write a newspaper article about something you want to accomplish 10 to 20 years from now as though it were already accomplished. Include some of the preparation necessary to accomplish it. Be creative.

7–2

ROOTS

Objective

To have the children research their heritage to become aware of their roots and to increase their sense of belonging and security.

Purpose

To promote a positive self-image.
To increase a sense of belonging.

Activities

1. Ask the children to research their roots (heritage) by interviewing their grandparents (or the oldest member in their family). (The child who is interviewing may write the information down, or the person being interviewed may write the information down, or a tape recorder may be used to have the information for a permanent record.) The information obtained should include:

   a. Place of birth; year of birth; family structure.

   b. What was life like when they were growing up? Discuss the history during that time. Include descriptions and stories about the clothes, politics, entertainment, diseases and remedies, transportation, songs, dance crazes, educational opportunities, and the like. Talk about how they coped with any problems they might have had.

   c. Look at family pictures of their grandparents' youth. (The children should be able to acquire further information by a spontaneous interchange during the interviews.)

2. Write reports on the countries, states, and cities of origin mentioned in the interview. (Include costumes, customs, and both past and present lifestyles.) Make information booklets which may be shared with the class.

3. Have a "Heritage Day." Ask the children to bring in some of the clothes, foods, musical instruments, songs, etc., of the time periods and the places mentioned in the "Heritage Interview." Invite the grandparents, parents, or guardians that have been involved in the project.

Note: *If families are separated by great distances, encourage communication by telephone or through the mail to explore the child's heritage. Supporting a sense of continuity and pride by encouraging communication between generations enriches each life, and can give a greater sense of security to all concerned.*

Reminder:

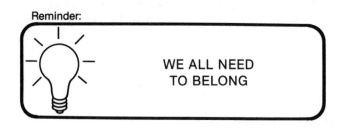

WE ALL NEED
TO BELONG

7–3

MOOD CHANGES

Objective

To help the children become more aware of what is going on inside of them (mood changes). To help them explore the effects their feelings have on the decisions they make.

Purpose

To develop a positive self-image.
To clarify personal attitudes and values.

Activities

Make a "feeling box" by following the directions given on the "Make a Feeling Box" activity sheet (7–3A).

> *Note: The rest of this exercise may be explained at the beginning of an ordinary school day and then integrated with the events of that day.*

1. Instruct the children to:
   a. Place this "feeling box" on their desks. As they become aware of their changing moods during the course of the day, they should rotate the face that reflects their present feeling toward the class.
   b. Keep a log of what happened to make the feelings change. What mood appeared most often?
   c. Ask: Does thinking about something that is not happening right now change your mood? Discuss
   d. Can your mood affect your outlook on life at that time? Does it affect your responses to other people? Discuss.

   Example: mood—sad; outlook—gloomy; behavior—depressed, withdrawn

> *Note:* **Explain that everyone has good and bad feelings. Give students permission and acceptance for all feelings.** Feelings **are neither right nor wrong. We are only responsible for our** behavior. **In order to grow or make changes, we first have to** recognize **what our feelings are.**
>
> **You may also make a ''feeling box'' and place it on your desk to participate in the exercise and share your feelings with the class.**

2. Discuss: When we are in different moods, may we choose *different* solutions to the *same* problem?

3. Discuss the importance of finding someone you trust with whom to share inner feelings. Have some students already found someone?

Reminder:

FEELINGS ARE OKAY

Making a "Feeling Box"

Materials

1. oaktag or cardboard
2. a pair of scissors
3. adhesive tape
4. marker
5. decorations (if desired)

Directions

1. Have each student cut a piece of oaktag or cardboard into a "T" shape with measurements as shown on the pattern (7–3B).

   a. Mark off four-inch sections as indicated in the illustration.

   b. Fold the oaktag along these lines to create a box shape.

   c. Tuck the tabs inside the box form.

   d. Use adhesive tape to fasten the pieces together.

2. Draw one of the "feeling faces" (mad, glad, sad, scared) on each of the four sides of the cube with marker. Or, if you choose, the four feeling faces shown on the "Feeling Faces" activity sheet (7–3C) may be duplicated for each student. The students may then cut the sheet of paper into four separate pictures and paste them on the four sides of the "feeling box."

3. To decorate: Make the boxes as elaborate as you wish. Use ribbons or caps on the tops, bow ties, earrings, etc.

4. The completed four-inch square box will look something like the one shown in the illustration.

The Feeling Box Pattern

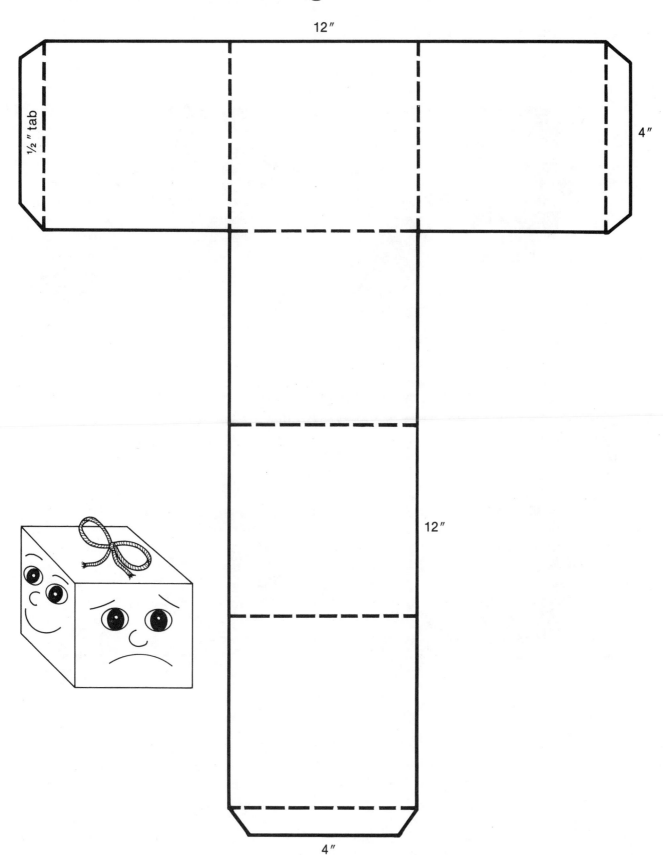

Feeling Faces

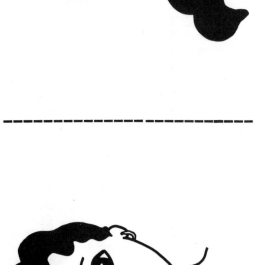

GLAD

MAD

SAD

SCARED

7–4

CHOICES AND CONSEQUENCES

Objective

To have the children recognize the need to make choices and accept consequences of those choices.

Purpose

To improve decision-making skills.
To improve coping skills.

Activities

1. To dramatize that *choices* have *unavoidable consequences* that affect our lives, explore the following exercise with the children: Your parents have gone out for the evening. You are home alone. Suddenly, you see flames coming from the kitchen. You have only *two minutes* to collect things you *value* to carry out of the house. What would you choose to take with you? What then, are some of the things you would *have* to leave behind?

2. To illustrate that making a choice may require *taking a stand*, ask the children the following:

   a. What is your favorite team, or song, or TV program?

   b. Does everyone in your family root for the same team, or like the same song or TV program?

   c. Does everyone in your class root for the same team, or like the same song or TV program?

   d. Do you sometimes change your mind to feel more comfortable in the group, even though you do not agree with them?

3. To illustrate the effects of peer pressure on one's self when making choices, do the following exercise:

   a. Put a long strip of masking tape on the floor. It will identify the degree of *commitment* to a decision:

   Example:

masking tape	10	5	1
	feel strongly for the issue	undecided	feel strongly against the issue

b. Ask a student to *take a stand* on an issue or make a choice in response to a dilemma or problem. The student will stand on that part of the masking tape line that indicates his or her position.

c. The rest of the students may try to "pressure" that student to change his or her mind by offering arguments or promises.

Example Issues

(1) Everyone has to try something to see for themselves.

(2) Girls should be able to do all of the same jobs as boys when they become adults.

(3) You are the star pitcher on your team. If your team wins today you will go into the playoffs. You are scheduled to pitch. Your best friend has two box seat tickets to your favorite professional baseball team's game today. He invited you to go to the game with him. Take a stand using the masking tape scale from 1 to 10.

(4) Your best friend is the student leader who has called a class "walk out" because of the lunch hour being shortened. The principal is aware of this, and has declared a three-day suspension for everyone who participates. Your parents will ground you for the weekend if you take part. Your friend will be upset if you don't join in. Take a stand (1 through 10).

The class may continue to talk about problems on which to *take a stand*. The children can discuss the feelings of being pressured. Did it have an effect on their commitment to the decision they originally made? Explore the issue of peer pressure and the decision to drink alcohol or smoke cigarettes.

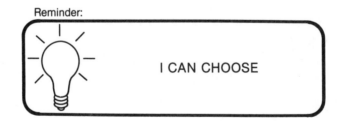

Reminder:

I CAN CHOOSE

7–5

RESOURCES FOR PROBLEM SOLVING

Objective

To help the children identify resources for help in solving problems.

Purpose

To improve coping skills.

Activities

1. Have the children make a list of people who can help them in a crisis—or who can help them to deal with "feeling" (emotional) problems.

   Examples:

friend	teacher	parents
counselor	doctor	clergyman
older sibling	hot-line worker	

2. Have the students find telephone numbers in the telephone directory for service organizations near them.

   Examples:

   The United Way

   Cerebral Palsy Association

   The Red Cross

   Alcoholics Anonymous

   Al-Anon

   Alateen

   A local hospital

   Poison Control Center

   Suicide Hotline

   Local mental health agency

3. Request literature from each organization and discuss the services offered. The class may prepare their own "Helping Hand" Directory with the information found, for future reference. It should be kept in an easily accessible place.

4. Have each student in the class take a piece of paper and write a real or invented problem on it, in any area of life, for which he or she would like to

receive help. Ask the children to fold the papers. Collect them in a box. Have someone pick a paper out of the box and read it to the class. Have the class decide where they can turn to find help for the problem. No *solutions* need be offered, just where *help* may be found.

Note: ***The students should not sign their names to the papers, as this may afford them with the opportunity to deal with a real problem and assist them in finding a solution, without revealing their identities.***

Reminder:

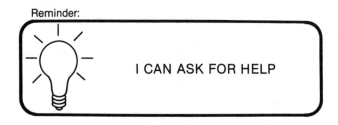

7–6

BRAINSTORMING

Objective

To familiarize the children with the *Brainstorming* technique (group effort) as a way to find solutions for specific problems.

Purpose

To improve coping skills.

Activity

Have each child write a problem on a piece of paper, which might be encountered now or in the future, that he or she may wish to discuss. Place it in the "computer box."

1. Select a problem from the box.
2. Pick a secretary to write the problem and the list of solutions that are offered, on the blackboard. (All solutions will be accepted without comment.)
3. When all solutions have been received, begin to explore each solution with the class for its positive and negative consequences.
4. Have the class vote on the most reasonable and helpful solution to the problem.
5. Place a star next to the solution that most of the students agree upon.
6. Have the secretary keep a record of the problems and the accepted solutions.
7. Make a cover for this "Booklet of Solutions." Leave it in a convenient place for further reference.

Following is a list of sample questions that you may suggest for problem solving:

SAMPLE QUESTIONS

1. Your friend has been drinking at a party. He wants to drive you home. What would you do?
2. When I visit one of my friends at his home, he offers me some beer from the refrigerator. I'm not sure if I want to drink alcohol. What should I do?
3. They were passing a "joint" (marijuana cigarette) around at a party. Everyone had tried it. I was the last one to try it. I really didn't want to try it, but I did. What can I do the next time?
4. A group of older boys in school are harassing a particular student every day after school. I don't think it's fair. What can I do to help without making enemies for myself?

5. I want to give a party. I don't plan to have alcohol. What can I do if someone else brings some to the party?

6. My parents and I do not agree on the use of alcohol. They feel it is "bad." I would like to have a glass of wine at family celebrations. What can I do?

7. My friend's father drinks a lot and hits him when he's drunk. What can I do to help? What can he do?

8. My sister has a date with a new boyfriend. He is obviously drunk when he arrives. They are going out to dinner. She tells me not to interfere when I bring the matter to her attention. What should I do?

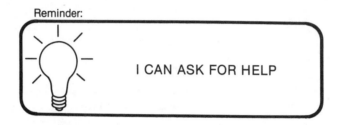

7–7

CIGARETTE SMOKING AND YOUR BODY

Objective

To have the children identify and discuss some physical effects of cigarette smoking on their bodies.

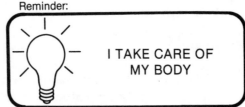

Reminder:

I TAKE CARE OF MY BODY

Purpose

To improve decision-making ability.
To clarify attitudes and values.

Activities

1. Review the Fact Sheets for Cigarette Smoking as shown in Appendix 2A.

2. Have the children research and report on topics related to cigarette smoking:

   a. The history of tobacco

   b. The tobacco industry

   c. The Surgeon General's Reports on Cigarette Smoking

   d. Diseases caused by cigarette smoking

3. It is a fact that the nicotine (poison) and carbon monoxide in cigarette smoke elevate blood pressure, and increase the heart rate and pulse rate causing the heart to work harder. To demonstrate an elevation in heart and pulse rate:

   a. Ask the children to sit quietly in their seats and relax for one minute.

   b. Assist the children in locating their pulses at the carotid artery under the jaw, at the middle of either side of the neck. (Instruct them to use a light touch so as not to cause a discomfort or interfere with the blood flow.)

   c. Count the beats for one minute with a clock or watch with a second hand.

   d. Instruct the children to jump "in place" for one minute, and then retake their pulses. Were there more beats this time?

   e. Are they also now aware of their hearts beating in their chests? Were they aware of it before the exercise? (Usually the answer is no.)

   f. Ask: What would it be like to have your heart work at that speed all the time? Why? Would it interfere with participation in athletic activities? Do many athletes smoke?

4. Request the Optioscopic Lung from your local American Cancer Society Office to view the healthy lung and the lung diseased by cigarette smoking.

7–8

CIGARETTE SMOKING AND
SOCIETAL ATTITUDES

Objective

To have the children become aware of the present attitudes in society towards smoking cigarettes.

Purpose

To improve decision-making skills.
To clarify personal values and attitudes.

Activities

1. Have the children monitor television programs and recent movies over a period of several days or more. Ask: Do you see anyone smoking cigarettes? (Actors now often create their characters without using the cigarette as a prop to project an image of sophistication, toughness, or power.)

2. Have the children make a list of ads on television that tell of the dangers of smoking. Ask:

    a. Was the presentor an actor, doctor, athlete, or politician?

    b. What were the main ideas expressed? List them and discuss them with the class.

3. Observe and report on public places that have "no smoking" areas (restaurants, planes, theatres, hospitals, and doctors' offices, to start).

4. Review the Surgeon General's Warnings found on each pack of cigarettes. (See activity sheet 6–7A.)

5. Ask the children to check how many newspaper want ads request that the applicant be a nonsmoker, and report this to the class. Discuss the effects of cigarette smoke on the nonsmokers in the area. (See the Smoking Fact Sheet in Appendix 2A.)

6. Explore the cost of cigarette smoking. Complete the "Paying the Price" activity sheet (7–8A).

    a. How much does a pack of cigarettes cost?

    b. If you have a one-pack-a-day "habit," how much money could it cost you for a week, a month, a year?

    c. Make a list of things you could buy if you did not spend the money on cigarettes.

7. Invite a person from the American Cancer Society, Lung Association, or Heart Association to speak to the class about the dangers of smoking.

8. Complete the "Words in the Pack" activity sheet (7–8B):

   a. Fill in the words to complete the sentences.

   b. Then find those words on the "Pack of Cigarettes" word search (7–8C).

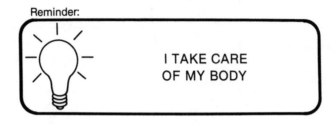

Reminder:

I TAKE CARE
OF MY BODY

Paying the Price

THE COST OF CIGARETTE SMOKING	IF I DO NOT SMOKE I CAN BUY:

1 pack of cigarettes costs

$ _____

_____

_____

1 pack of cigarettes per day for a

week costs $ _____

_____

_____

_____

1 pack of cigarettes per day for a

month costs $ _____

_____

_____

_____

1 pack of cigarettes per day for a

year costs $ _____

_____

_____

1 pack of cigarettes per day for 5

years costs $ _____

_____

I CAN CHOOSE

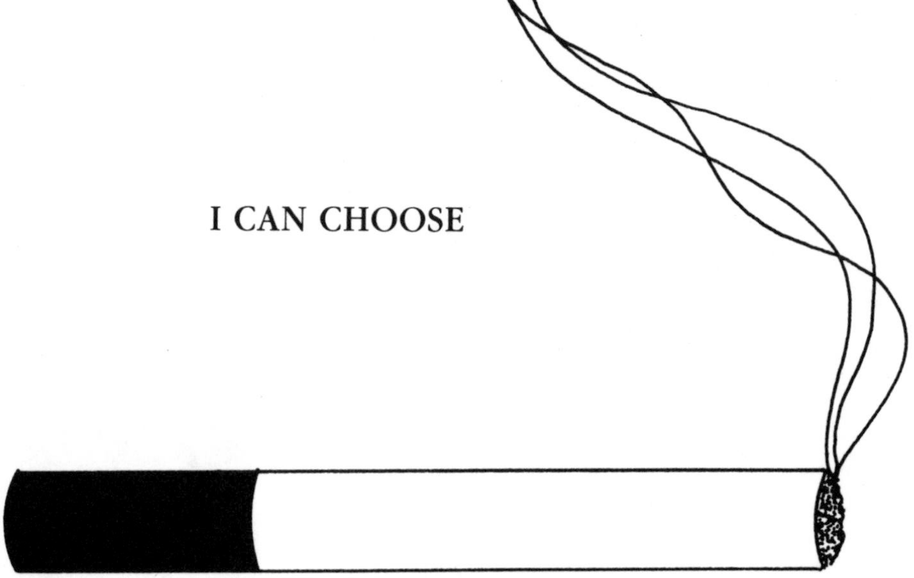

GOING UP IN SMOKE.

Words in the Pack

Complete these sentences using words found on the pack of cigarettes below.

1. Cigarette smoking causes stains on your _____.

2. Cigarette smoking can cause _____ cancer.

3. Cigarette smoking makes you short of _____.

4. Cigarettes are made of _____ leaves.

5. The Surgeon General has issued the latest report on the _____ of cigarette smoking.

6. The poison that replaces the _____ in the blood is carbon monoxide.

7. A person _____ his or her environment when smoking.

8. _____ are the cancer-causing substances in cigarettes.

9. There are often nonsmoking sections in _____.

10. The discomfort a person feels when he or she stops smoking is called _____.

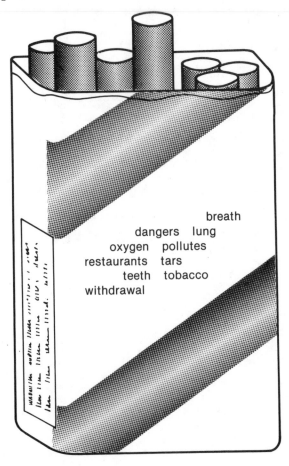

breath
dangers   lung
oxygen   pollutes
restaurants   tars
teeth   tobacco
withdrawal

Pack of Cigarettes

Find these words in the word search below. The words can be found horizontally and vertically.

BREATH	POLLUTES	TEETH
DANGERS	RESTAURANT	TARS
LUNG	TOBACCO	OXYGEN
	WITHDRAWAL	

```
Y M T A R S B C T L O R W
X T O X Y G E N E U X E I
B S B R E A T H E N Y S T
W R A F H Q R S T G K T H
V T C O A L T A H V E A D
C P C T P O L L U T E S R
U Q O U V W X Z X K L M A
T B T R E A T S O W I T W
D A A D A N G E R S D R A
S M R E S T A U R A N T L
```

7–9

ATTITUDES ABOUT ALCOHOL

Objective

To have the children explore personal, family, and community attitudes towards the use of alcohol.

Purpose

To clarify attitudes and values.
To improve decision making.

Activities

Note: You may examine your own attitudes privately using these exercises.

---

1. Have the children make a family tree going back to their great-grandparents. Ask: Can you identify attitudes in your family concerning alcohol? (used in religious observances only; for celebrations only; for every night "beer blasts," or whatever applies). How do you think these attitudes affect *your* attitude toward alcohol today?

2. Have each child write five words that immediately come to mind when he or she hears the word "drunk." What *attitude* do you think it shows? (fearful, funny, embarrassed, sad, indifferent).

3. Ask: If you were a parent, what rules would you impose on your children concerning the use of alcohol?

4. Have the children complete the sentences in the "Thinking It Through" activity sheet (7–9A). (The class may continue to create sentences to explore this topic.)

Reminder:

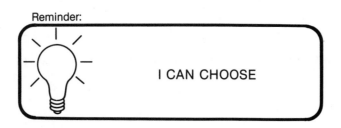
I CAN CHOOSE

Thinking It Through

1. When I see someone drunk on the street I _____

   _____ .

2. When other kids call me a "baby" because I won't drink a can of beer, I feel _____

   _____ .

3. Some of my friends will have a 4th of July party. If there is any liquor there, I will _____

   _____ .

4. If someone in my family had a drinking problem, I would _____

   _____ .

5. If I was very unhappy about something, and I did not feel comfortable talking to someone at

   home, I could talk to _____

   _____ .

6. I would feel _____ if my parents saw me drinking a can of beer.

7. When television commercials show a baseball star laughing and drinking with his buddies, I

   think _____

   _____ .

8. I've heard a lot of famous people talk about being an "alcoholic." They look okay to me.

   That makes me think that _____

   _____ .

9. When I get older, if I am a host of a party at which liquor is served, I will tell my guests ____

   _____ .

10. When an adult drinks only soft drinks at a wedding celebration, I think _____

   _____ .

7–10

ALCOHOL AND THE BODY

Objective

To teach the students more about the drug, alcohol.

Purpose

To increase knowledge about the drug, alcohol.
To improve decision-making and coping skills.

Activities

1. Have students define these words which are related to alcohol:

   absorption   intoxication   circulation   crutch   rehabilitation
   depressant   sedation   cirrhosis   moderation   alcoholism
   ingestion   oxidation   excretion   addiction   abstinence

2. Review the Fact Sheets for Alcohol. (See Appendix 2B–1 to 2B–5.)

3. Discuss some of the occasions at which alcohol may be used:

   a. As part of a *religious ritual*. (Have the children name some religions that use wine as part of their ceremonies.)

   b. *As part of a meal*, as the beverage enhancing the food. (Tell the children that when alcohol is taken by adults in small amounts, it stimulates the gastric juices and can enhance the meal. When it is taken in large amounts, it irritates the digestive system.)

   c. *For socialization* (to produce a feeling of relaxation).

      Discuss the fact that alcohol is a *sedative drug*. When taken by adults in *moderation*, it can create a calming effect. In excess, it impairs normal functioning.

4. Have the students learn the pathway alcohol takes through the body, as shown in "The Body with Alcohol Present" (7–10A).

5. Reproduce the "Alcohol in the Body" (7–10B) activity sheet for each student. Direct them to

   a. Trace the pathway of alcohol through the body with a blue pencil or crayon.

   b. Label and color in red the organs of the body that are affected by alcohol.

Reminder:

I TAKE CARE
OF MY BODY

The Body with Alcohol Present

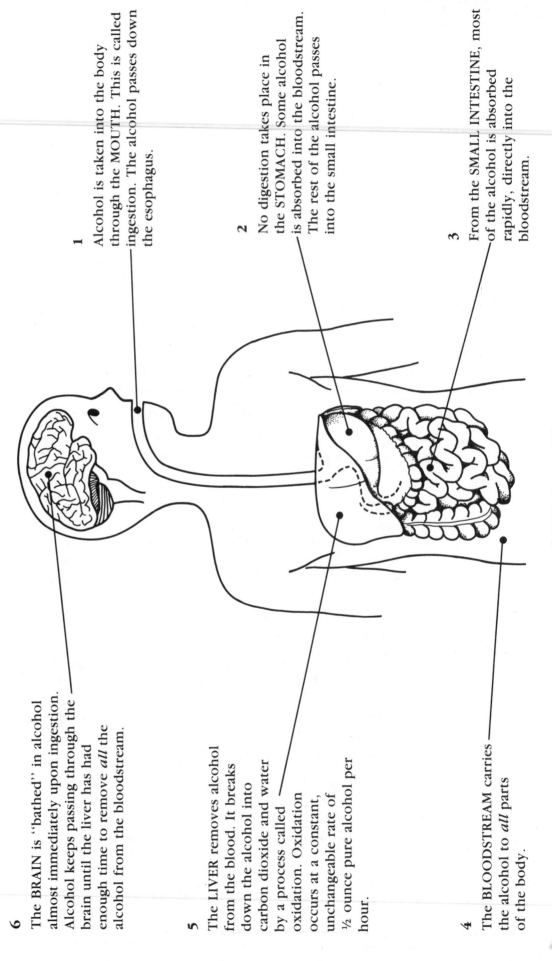

1
Alcohol is taken into the body through the MOUTH. This is called ingestion. The alcohol passes down the esophagus.

2
No digestion takes place in the STOMACH. Some alcohol is absorbed into the bloodstream. The rest of the alcohol passes into the small intestine.

3
From the SMALL INTESTINE, most of the alcohol is absorbed rapidly, directly into the bloodstream.

6
The BRAIN is "bathed" in alcohol almost immediately upon ingestion. Alcohol keeps passing through the brain until the liver has had enough time to remove *all* the alcohol from the bloodstream.

5
The LIVER removes alcohol from the blood. It breaks down the alcohol into carbon dioxide and water by a process called oxidation. Oxidation occurs at a constant, unchangeable rate of ½ ounce pure alcohol per hour.

4
The BLOODSTREAM carries the alcohol to *all* parts of the body.

Alcohol in the Body

1. Use a blue pencil or crayon to trace the pathway of alcohol through the body.

2. Use a red pencil or crayon to label and color the organs of the body that are affected by alcohol.

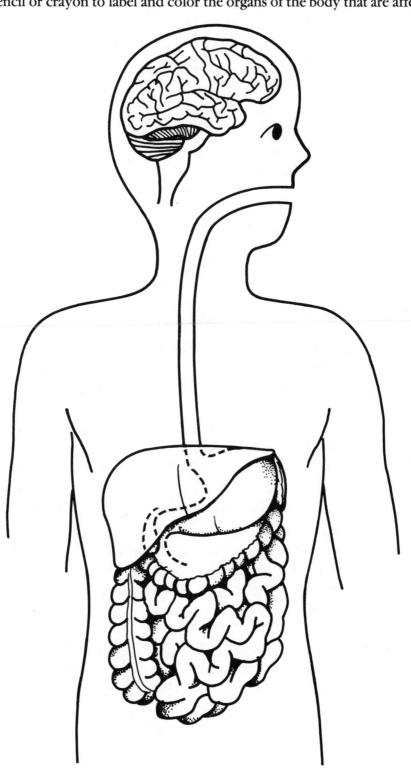

7–11

THE BLOOD-ALCOHOL CONCENTRATION WHEEL

Objective

To have the students learn more about the effects of alcohol upon a person by using the "Blood Alcohol Concentration (BAC) Wheel."

Purpose

To increase knowledge about the effects of the drug, alcohol.
To improve decision-making skills.

Activities

1. To make the BAC Wheel:

   a. Follow the directions given on the two "BAC Wheel" activity sheets (7–11A and 7–11B).

2. To use the BAC Wheel:

   As an example: If you had four average-sized drinks of beer, wine, or mixed drinks:

   a. Line up the number 4 in the number of drinks row with the outer ring, which shows your weight.

   b. Read the figure which appears in the upper window. This is your BAC if you have taken the 4 drinks within a quarter hour.

   c. By looking at the bottom window, you can determine what your BAC would be with the passage of time. Experiment with other combinations. What would be your BAC if you weighed 40 pounds more, or if you had 2 drinks or 6 drinks in one hour?

Note: Since alcohol is absorbed directly into the bloodstream and transported rapidly throughout the body, the percentage of alcohol present in the body can be obtained by a breath test or a blood test. The degree of intoxication and some of its predictable effects can then be anticipated.

---

3. To determine probable effects of feeling and behavior:

   a. Use the BAC Wheel to measure the degree of intoxication; for example, .01, .10, or .15 percent. (Review the factors which influence the speed at which the alcohol is absorbed, found in Appendix 2B–1, item 6. Review the other factors that may influence how alcohol affects the individual, as shown in Appendix 2B–1, item 7.)

b. Explore the probable behavior which would be visible at the degree of intoxication as shown in the ''Visible Signs of Intoxication'' activity sheet (7–11C).

Reminder:

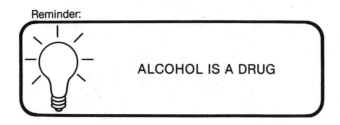

ALCOHOL IS A DRUG

BAC Wheel

Part 1

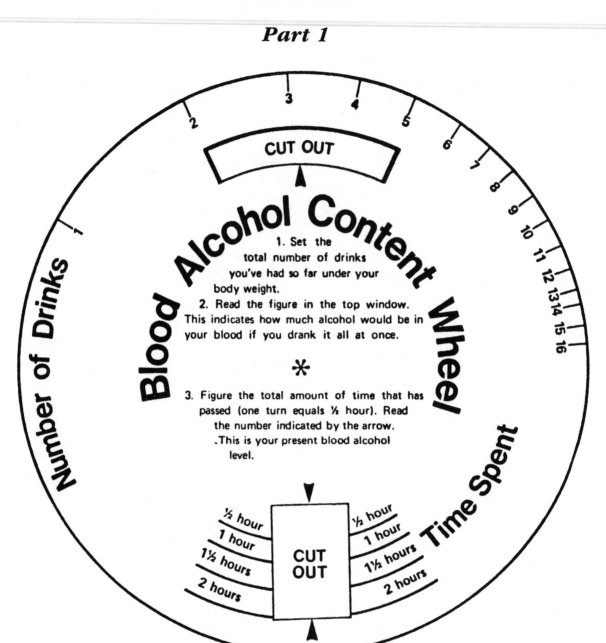

CUT OUT

Number of Drinks

Blood Alcohol Content Wheel

1. Set the total number of drinks you've had so far under your body weight.

2. Read the figure in the top window. This indicates how much alcohol would be in your blood if you drank it all at once.

*

3. Figure the total amount of time that has passed (one turn equals ½ hour). Read the number indicated by the arrow. This is your present blood alcohol level.

Time Spent

½ hour
1 hour
1½ hours
2 hours

CUT OUT

½ hour
1 hour
1½ hours
2 hours

2 3 4 5 6 7 8 9 10 11 12 13 14 15 16

1. Paste each page onto cardboard or manila paper.
2. Trim around each circle.
3. Use a razor to cut the two sections marked "CUT OUT."
4. Put the smaller circle on top of the larger one, carefully fastening them together at the stars (centers) with a paper fastener.

Source: Reprinted from Peter Finn and Judith Platt, *Alcohol and Alcohol Safety*, volume 2. Washington, D.C.: U.S. Government Printing Office, 1972.

BAC Wheel

Part 2

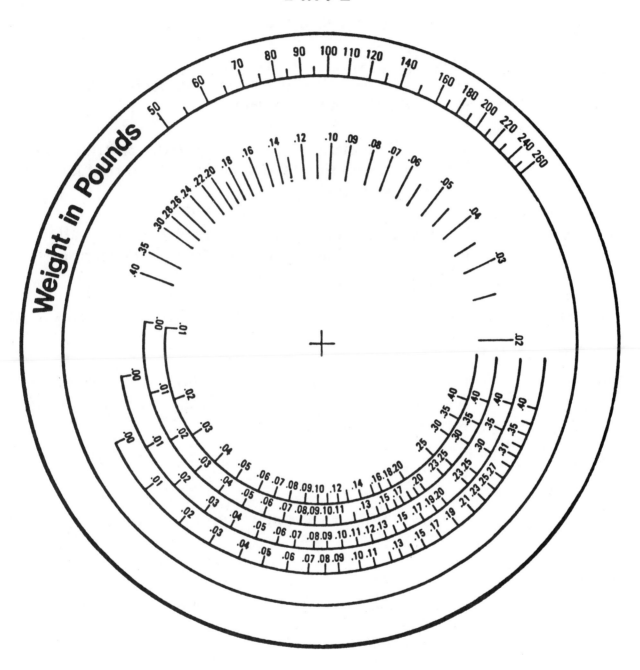

Source: Reprinted from Peter Finn and Judith Platt, *Alcohol and Alcohol Safety,* volume 2. Washington, D.C.: U.S. Government Printing Office, 1972.

Visible Signs of Intoxication

BAC	Effects on Feeling and Behavior
.01–.04%	Usually no apparent changes in behavior. More relaxed; minor impairment of judgment and memory.
.05–.08%	Walking, talking, and hand movements become more clumsy. Present "feeling" or mood becomes more pronounced (sad, happy, angry).
.08–.10%	Speech, judgment, balance affected. Blurred vision. Slower reaction time. (.10% is considered drunken driving in most states.)
.10–.15%	Judgment, memory, and self-control are further affected: irresponsible behavior evident. There is a decrease in the sense of pain. Speech is slurred.
.15–.20%	Behavior greatly affected. Lack of motor controls; mental confusion.
.20–.30%	Unable to perform tasks. Confused or dazed state. Unconsciousness may occur. All physical and mental abilities *severely* impaired.
.30 plus	Unconscious. Death is possible.
.40–.50%	The breathing process may stop functioning.

© 1986 by Prentice-Hall, Inc.

NOTE:

- Very rapid (gulping) drinking of *large amounts* of alcohol in a *short period* of time can stop breathing reflex and cause death.
- Mixing alcohol with other drugs can prove fatal.

7–12

THE DISEASE OF ALCOHOLISM

Objective

To have the students become aware of the disease of alcoholism and its effects.

Purpose

To increase knowledge about the drug, alcohol.
To improve decision-making skills.
To clarify personal values and attitudes.

Activities

1. Have the students research and report on an alcohol-related issue:

   Suggestions:

   Teenage drinking

   Drinking and driving

   Alcoholics Anonymous

   Al-Anon and Alateen

   Alcohol use and violence

2. Have the students review the "Alcoholism Fact Sheet," (7–12A).

3. Invite a professional in the field of alcoholism treatment or prevention, or Alcoholics Anonymous, Al-Anon or Alateen to speak with the class.

4. Unscramble the words in the "Bumper Stickers" activity sheet (7–12B).

5. Have the students complete the "All About Alcohol" crossword puzzle (7–12C).

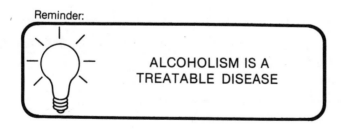

Reminder:

ALCOHOLISM IS A
TREATABLE DISEASE

Alcoholism Fact Sheet

GETTING SICK

1. Abuse of the drug, alcohol, can lead to the disease of *alcoholism*.

2. Alcoholism is a chronic, progressive, and potentially fatal disease.

3. It is an addiction characterized by three criteria: A *tolerance* develops. It now requires more and more of the drug to give the desired effect. *Dependency* occurs when the body and/or the mind become so accustomed to the presence of the drug and its effects, that unpleasant physical and emotional symptoms result when the drug is stopped, which are called *withdrawal* symptoms.

4. Drinking alcohol becomes the *most* important thing in the alcoholic's life, taking up *more* and *more* time and energy. Essential daily functions begin to be neglected.

5. The inability to function effectively (due to the use of this sedative drug), brings on many *problems* for the addicted person in all areas of his or her life: family, job, school, money, health and legal.

6. This abusive drinking can lead to serious *damage* to the body organs and their functions, especially the brain and the liver.

GETTING WELL

1. Alcoholism is a *treatable* disease.

2. While there is *no cure*, it can be arrested. A person with this disease can return to a happy, useful, *drug-free* life.

3. There are many people who are specially trained to help people with drinking problems, when they want to begin the process of getting well. There are *treatment centers* available to meet the needs of alcoholics.

4. *Alcoholics Anonymous* is a fellowship of men and women who come together to offer each other hope, experience, and support to live a productive life, free of the drug, alcohol.

5. The *Al-Anon Family Groups* (*Al-Anon* and *Alateen*) are fellowships of wives, husbands, children, relatives, and friends of problem drinkers. Through the group experience, they share their strength and hope with each other in order to understand and overcome the problems resulting from this family disease. (The alcoholic need not be a member of Alcoholics Anonymous for the family members to participate in Al-Anon or Alateen.)

6. After the alcoholic has successfully stopped drinking alcohol, he or she *cannot drink alcohol again*, without activating their disease. (People with allergies to certain substances, like eggs, chocolate, penicillin, cannot use *those* substances without serious bodily consequences, either.)

> *Note: A number for each of those organizations can be found in your local telephone directory in most areas of the country or in the directory at the end of the book.*

Bumper Stickers

Change each bumper sticker's spacing of letters to get the message across.

1.

AL COHOLI SAD RUG

2.

ICA NLE ARNTO FA CE
MYPR OBLEMS

3.

ALC OHOL ISMIS ADIS EASE

4.

IC ANM AKEC HOICES

5.

ON LYSICK PEO PLE
NE   ED   DR   UGS

1. _____

_____

2. _____

_____

3. _____

_____

4. _____

_____

5. _____

_____

Name _____

Date _____

All About Alcohol

Complete this crossword puzzle using the words found on the bottles and cans.

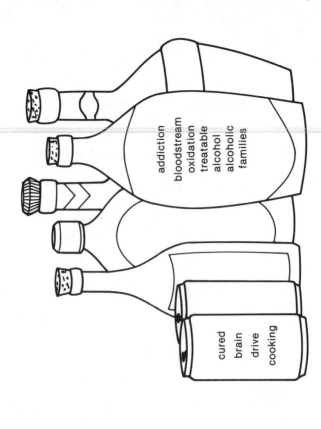

Words on bottles:
addiction
bloodstream
oxidation
treatable
alcohol
alcoholic
families

Words on cans:
cured
brain
drive
cooking

ACROSS

1. The physical dependence upon a drug for which we develop a tolerance is called an _____.
3. The _____ carries alcohol to the brain.
7. Al-Anon is a self-help group for the _____ of alcoholics.
8. The most abused drug in our culture is _____.
9. Alcohol is used in _____ to flavor sauces.
10. Alcoholism cannot be _____, but it can be arrested.

DOWN

2. Alcoholism is a _____ disease.
3. The body organ most sensitive to alcohol is the _____.
4. The process by which alcohol is broken down and removed from the body is called _____.
5. When adults drink alcohol, they should not _____ a car.
6. A person addicted to the drug alcohol is an _____.

© 1986 by Prentice-Hall, Inc.

7–13

POSITIVE PEER PRESSURE

Objective

To help the students become aware of their "power" to influence others, and to have the children become more knowledgeable about personal growth issues and substance abuse prevention through their research, preparation, and presentation to the children in lower grade levels.

Purpose

To improve self-image.
To clarify personal values and attitudes.

Activities

1. Define the role of "peer counselor" (student-helpers). Explore the positive effects of teaching younger students (increased self-esteem, knowledge, and sensitivity).

2. Talk about the talents that each person possesses. Ask for volunteers to use those talents to help in this project. *All* class members will participate. (It may be necessary for you to help some children recognize their abilities and encourage them to join a team.)

   a. The class may form groups to prepare presentations for students in any grade, K through 5. The children will use their talents to be on one of the teams mentioned below:

      (1) script writers

      (2) set designers

      (3) puppet creators

      (4) puppet actors

      (5) master of ceremonies

      (6) advertising specialists to prepare announcements, develop brochures and programs with important information about substance abuse.

3. Have the class create a "TV set," from which to present their skits. (Follow the directions given on the "TV Set" activity sheet (7–13A).)

4. Have the class review information found in this book for students in one of the lower grades. The children may prepare skits to include the information. The children should be encouraged to develop original material, adding current information. (Use paper-plate puppets or paper-cup puppets and design with the students.)

5. Prepare puppet shows dealing with expressing feelings. (Use colored balloons with faces painted on them to show emotions: red—anger; blue—sad; green—envy; yellow—happy/sunny; white—fear; etc.) See the "Performing Puppets" activity sheet (7–13B). Paper plate or paper cup puppets may also be used.

> Note: *Allow the younger students in the audience to interact and respond to the puppets.*

Reminder:

I AM UNIQUE

TV Set

Materials

a large cardboard box
a pair of scissors
glue
paint or self-stick vinyl

Directions

1. Cut off the panels from the open end of the large box.
2. On the opposite side of the opening, cut a square area for a TV screen.
3. Paint or cover the box to complete the appearance of a TV.
4. Draw knobs under the TV screen. (Door hardware can be also used.)
5. The TV set can be placed on a desk or table for easy viewing. The puppet managers can stand behind the TV set.

Performing Puppets

1. **Use:** Balloons, magic marker, string, small piece of cloth or a handkerchief.

Directions: Use appropriately colored balloons to correspond with a particular emotion. Draw a face, hold string, and cover hand with a draped handkerchief or cloth.

yellow—
happy/sunny

white-
fear

red—
angry

cloth →

hand →

or

2. **Use:** Paper cups, magic marker or crayons, tongue depressors and handkerchief.

Directions: Use paper cups turned upside down. Draw faces with magic marker. Insert a hand if it is small enough, or attach to a tongue depressor with paste. Hold with hand covered with cloth.

or

3. **Use:** Paper plates, magic marker or crayons, tongue depressors and handkerchief.

Directions: Staple two paper plates face to face. (Draw faces with magic marker.) Tape tongue depressor or stick, which had been inserted within the paper plates, so it will not slip. Hold with hand covered with cloth.

APPENDICES

APPENDIX 1A:
SLOGANS AND REMINDERS

At the end of each activity, a slogan/reminder is provided for you to use with the children. Frequent repetition of these simple reminders (verbal or written) will reinforce their important concepts and strengthen their effect.

Examples:

Reminder:

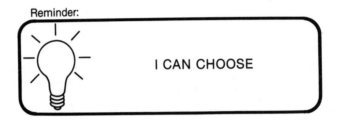

I CAN CHOOSE

These reminders can be used during times of stress. They should be readily available to replace negative ideas with positive thoughts and assist in defining a particular need or conflict.

Reminders

1. I AM UNIQUE
2. FEELINGS ARE OKAY
3. I AM RESPONSIBLE FOR WHAT I DO
4. I CAN CHOOSE
5. I CAN HELP
6. I CAN ASK FOR HELP
7. WE ALL NEED TO BELONG
8. I TAKE CARE OF MY BODY
9. ONLY SICK PEOPLE NEED DRUGS
10. ALCOHOL IS A DRUG
11. I CAN SAY NO
12. ADDICTION IS A TREATABLE DISEASE

APPENDIX 1B:
CONDITIONS FOR EFFECTIVE DRUG EDUCATION

In the area of drug prevention education in the schools, there must be an atmosphere of good communication, consistency of expectations and limit-setting, and the credibility of an accurately informed staff, knowledgeable in drug information and identification of symptoms of drug use. The specific information on commonly abused drugs was included in a separate section to be easily accessible for the teacher's use at any grade level. This information can be provided to the students at the appropriate "teachable moment," such as

1. When a child asks specific questions
2. When the teacher has heard misinformation presented
3. As part of a lesson that includes attention to personal growth, development, and health issues

(Addiction studies have shown that when lessons were taught, focusing primarily on drug *information*, a rise in the use of drugs was noted due, perhaps, to an increase in curiosity, risk-taking, and sensation seeking.)

APPENDIX 1C:
SIGNS OF DRUG INVOLVEMENT

School Behaviors	Psychological Symptoms
Poor grades from a formerly good student	Unusual overactivity and talkativeness
Skipping class	Depression and suicidal talk or behavior
Truancy	Mood swings
General loss of interest in school	Confusion
Disinterest in sports or hobbies previously enjoyed	Anxiety
Confrontations with school authorities	Hallucinations
	Apathy
	Excuses and rationalizations

Social Behaviors	Physical Symptoms
Changes in personality and behavior	Deterioration of physical appearance and lack of grooming
Changes in friends	Loss of physical coordination
Association with people known to use drugs	Eye changes (glassy, dilated or constricted pupils; reddening of the whites of the eyes)
Secret phone conversations with strangers	Dreamy, blank expression
Withdrawal from family activities	Wearing long-sleeved garments (to hide possible needle marks)
Acting-out behavior (temper flareups, overt hostility)	Wearing sunglasses at inappropriate times to hide eye signs
Frequent borrowing of money	Empty beer cans, liquor bottles, spoons, pipes, needles that might be used to administer drugs
Disappearance of money or drugs from the home	Slurred speech
Frequently evasive or lies about activities	Change in sleep patterns
Unexplained presence in out-of-the-way places (garage, basement, storage areas)	Weight loss or gain
	Change in appetite
	Restlessness or excitability

Note: *Several of the above symptoms, that may be noticed for a period of time,* could *be an indication of drug use. Further investigation might be warranted.*

APPENDIX 2A:
CIGARETTE SMOKING FACT SHEET

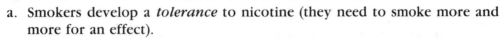

1. *Cigarette smoking is addictive*; it fulfills these three criteria:

   a. Smokers develop a *tolerance* to nicotine (they need to smoke more and more for an effect).

   b. Smokers become *dependent* on it (they *need* it to feel comfortable).

   c. Smokers suffer *withdrawal* symptoms (physical and psychological discomfort when they try to stop smoking).

2. There are hundreds of chemical substances in cigarette smoke. Three of the most damaging are:

   a. *Tars*—damage delicate lung tissue and are considered the main cancer-causing agent in cigarette smoke.

   b. *Nicotine*—a poison found only in tobacco leaves. It can be extracted as a colorless, oily transparent liquid and used in solution as an insecticide. One drop of pure nicotine can be fatal to humans.

      (1) It is a powerful stimulant to the brain and central nervous system that "hits" the brain within four seconds. Like the drug, alcohol, after it initially stimulates, it has a *depressant* effect.

      (2) Nicotine constricts (narrows) the blood vessels, cutting down the flow of blood and oxygen throughout your body. Your heart has to pump harder, thus increasing the chance of heart disease. It raises the blood pressure and also narrows bronchioles (air passageways) in the lungs, also depriving the body of some oxygen.

   c. *Carbon monoxide*—replaces needed oxygen in your red blood cells. Even after one stops smoking, carbon monoxide stays in the bloodstream for hours, depriving the body of oxygen until the oxygen level in your blood returns to normal. Carbon monoxide is a waste product of cigarette smoking and also of gasoline engines.

3. Some of the diseases caused by cigarette smoking are:

   a. chronic bronchitis (inflammation of the bronchi which are the breathing tubes in the lungs)

   b. laryngitis (inflammation of the throat)

   c. emphysema (a degenerative lung disease that destroys breathing capacity)

   d. and it is a contributing factor in cancer of the lungs, mouth, and esophagus.

Note: Cigarette smoking is the major single cause of cancer deaths in the United States (the U.S. Surgeon General's Report 1982).

4. Smoking cigarettes stains the *teeth*, reduces the efficiency of the body's ability to *taste* and *smell*, and increases the process of *wrinkling* of the skin (especially around the eyes).

5. The effects of some medication taken by a person may be increased, decreased, or cancelled out by smoking.

6. Cigarette smoking by pregnant women may cause harm to the fetus (see Surgeon General's warning).

7. Cigarette smoke pollutes the air in enclosed places, which also affects the nonsmokers present.

8. Smoke from an idle cigarette contains at least as much tar and nicotine as inhaled smoke (American Lung Association).

9. Chewing tobacco may lead to cancer of the mouth and to an addiction because of the nicotine which is absorbed through the mouth's lining.

10. It is generally accepted that ''peer pressure'' encourages many young people between the ages of 10 and 18 to begin experimenting with smoking (American Cancer Society).

11. When a person quits smoking, the body begins to repair some of the damage caused by the cigarette smoking.

Peer Pressure

APPENDIX 2B–1:
ALCOHOL FACT SHEET

1. *Alcohol is a drug* which affects the way the body naturally functions. It is a depressant drug that slows the body processes.

2. It is the oldest and most abused drug in the world.

3. There are predictable, though varying, physical effects upon everyone who drinks alcohol. (This is why the law has set a specific blood alcohol level for defining drunkenness while driving.)

4. It is this drug which is the intoxicating ingredient present in many substances (including wine, beer, rye, vodka, gin, rum, most cough medicines, some mouthwashes, cooking extracts, and some over-the-counter sleeping medicines).

5. Alcohol affects many of the body organs and their functions. (See Appendices 2B–2, 2B–3 and 2B–4.)

6. Factors which influence the speed at which the alcohol is absorbed include:

    a. the presence of *food* in the stomach (*decreases* the speed of absorption).

    b. the use of *carbonated beverages* with the alcohol (*increases* the speed of absorption).

    c. the *concentration* (proof) of the alcohol used.

       100% alcohol = 200 proof = strong poison

       50% alcohol = 100 proof

       43% alcohol = 86 proof

7. Other factors that may influence how alcohol affects the individual include:

    a. Amount of alcohol intake.

    b. Body weight.

    c. Age (children and the elderly are more sensitive).

    d. Previous drinking experience. (If one develops a tolerance, it takes more and more of the drug to get the desired effect.)

    e. The presence of other drugs in the system.

    f. The general health of the individual.

8. One who becomes addicted to the drug is called an *alcoholic*, and suffers from the disease of *alcoholism*.

ALCOHOL'S EFFECT ON THE BRAIN

The brain is the control center of the body:

1. It is the organ most affected by the presence of alcohol.

2. Alcohol is a drug that depresses the central nervous system, thus reducing the activity of the brain.

3. Alcohol arrives in the brain almost as soon as it is consumed.

4. The bloodstream carries alcohol to the brain.

5. It keeps circulating through the brain until the liver has had time to change (oxidize) all of the alcohol into carbon dioxide and water for release from the body. (The liver can only break down one-half ounce of pure alcohol per hour). During all this period, the brain remains intoxicated.

6. Exactly how soon the brain becomes affected depends on how quickly the alcohol passes from the stomach into the small intestines. (See Appendix 2B–1, item 6.)

7. It affects the higher functions of the brain—judgment, learning, and behavioral control. It then affects vision, coordination, and speech.

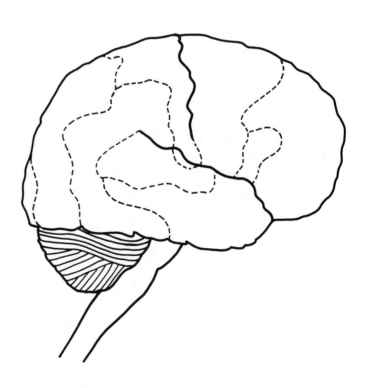

APPENDIX 2B–3:
ALCOHOL'S EFFECT ON THE LIVER

The liver is the body's chemical factory:

1. It helps us digest our food.

2. It also acts as a cleansing station, deactivating the poisonous effects of alcohol, medicines, and other drugs, so they lose their harmful effects on the body.

3. All the alcohol absorbed from the stomach and the small intestines is carried directly to the liver through the bloodstream.

4. *Oxidation* is the process by which approximately 95 percent of the alcohol is changed to carbon dioxide and water for elimination from the body. A small amount of alcohol is released, unchanged, through sweat, breath, and urine.

5. Only the liver can start the process of breaking down alcohol in the body. It does this only at a *constant, unchangeable* rate of *one-half ounce* of pure alcohol per hour (12 ounces of beer, 4 ounces of wine, 1 ½ ounce of 86 proof whiskey all contain the same amount of alcohol).

6. There is *no drug, food* or *exercise* that will increase the speed at which the liver breaks down the alcohol.

7. The "overload" of alcohol that the liver cannot deal with immediately, *continues to circulate* throughout the body within the bloodstream, affecting the brain and other organs.

8. With the intake of excessive amounts of alcohol, the liver "concentrates" on removing the alcohol from the blood, and "neglects" its other jobs or functions.

9. The liver becomes too busy metabolizing (breaking down) the alcohol to manufacture and release glucose (sugar) into the bloodstream. Glucose is the primary source of energy that the brain cells use.

10. Excessive use of alcohol can lead to liver damage.

Diseases of the Liver

1. *Fatty liver* is the mildest form of liver disease which results when there is a high intake of alcohol, and the liver neglects the breakdown of fat. At this point, if alcohol intake is stopped, the liver is able to return to normal.

2. *Hepatitis* is the next stage of damage if drinking continues. This indicates the inflammation of liver cells.

3. *Cirrhosis* is the most severe, often fatal, form of liver disease. All functions of the liver begin to fail. The excess alcohol kills the cells and they are replaced by scar tissue.

4. *Liver failure*, as a result of cirrhosis, causes the following:

   a. An accumulation throughout the body of toxic (poisonous) products that were usually broken down in the liver.

   b. The sugar level in the blood falls because glucose is no longer produced, thus depriving the brain of nutrients.

   c. Blood clotting substances usually produced by the liver decrease, and the danger of massive bleeding becomes likely.

   d. Kidneys begin to fail.

Complete liver failure is fatal.

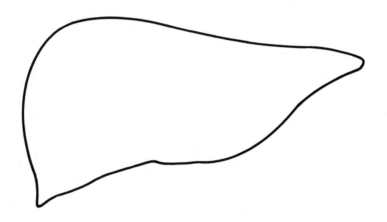

APPENDIX 2B–4:
ALCOHOL'S EFFECT ON THE STOMACH

In the stomach, alcohol promotes the flow of gastric juices.

1. Used in moderation, as a beverage with meals, alcohol may increase the appetite and enhance the meal.

2. In larger amounts, it interferes with digestion and causes irritation to the esophagus and the stomach lining.

3. Most food stays at least one hour in the stomach during the process of digestion. Alcohol *does not* require digestion in the stomach. Some of it is absorbed directly from the stomach into the bloodstream before it passes into the small intestines.

4. The presence of food in the stomach (especially proteins and fats) slows down this passage to the small intestines.

In the small intestines, alcohol is absorbed directly into the bloodstream, rapidly and completely.

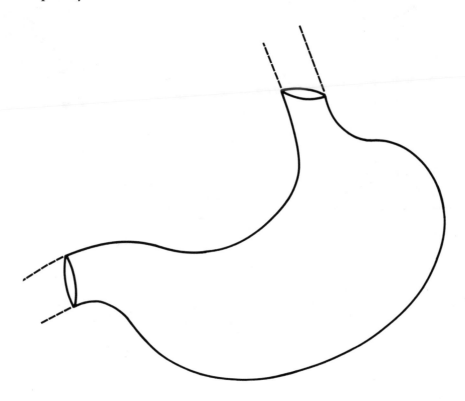

Each container has the same amount of alcohol:

1 drink = 4 oz. of wine
12 oz. of beer

1 oz. of 86 proof liquor

APPENDIX 2C
SEDATIVES

This group of drugs *depresses the central nervous system* and *slows the body processes.* There are two main groups of sedative medications: *barbiturates* and *tranquilizers.* MIXING THESE DRUGS WITH ALCOHOL CAN PROVE FATAL!

Drugs

Barbiturates—Nembutal, Seconal, Amytal, Phenobarbital Tuinal

Methaqualone—Quaalude, Mequin, Parest

Tranquilizers—Valium, Librium

Alcohol

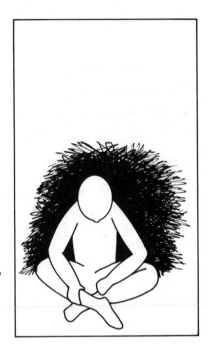

Street Names

Yellow jackets, reds, red devils, red birds, blues, blue heaven, purple hearts, tooeys, rainbow, ludes, barbs, downs

Medical Use

Anti-convulsant, relief of tension and anxiety, induce sleep, reduce symptoms of alcohol withdrawal

Route of Administration

Ingestion, injection

Effects of Barbiturates

- Relaxation of body's muscles
- Intoxication appears similar to that of alcohol (without the odor of alcohol present)
- Staggering and stumbling movements; slurred speech
- Drowsiness

Effect of Tranquilizers

- Calms the person's emotions without interfering with the ability to remain alert and think clearly

---

Note: Abusers of stimulants and hallucinogens may take sedatives to calm down. Sedatives are physically *and* psychologically *addictive. Withdrawal from these drugs should be done under medical supervision.*

APPENDIX 2D:
STIMULANTS

A stimulant is a drug that *increases alertness, activity, and excitement by speeding up the body's processes.*

Drugs

Amphetamines, cocaine, ritalin, caffeine

Street Names

Ups, bennies, whites, Christmas trees, uppers, dex, hearts, speed, black beauties

Medical Use

To treat overweight; to treat depression; cocaine can be used as a local anesthetic in eye, ear, nose, and throat surgery; for the treatment of narcolepsy (uncontrollable falling asleep during daily activities)

Route of Administration

Injection, inhalation, ingestion

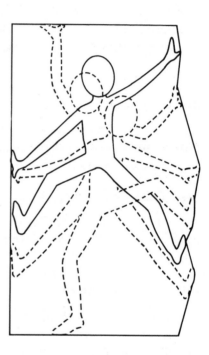

Effects

- Speed up the body's processes
- Decrease in appetite
- Dryness of the mouth
- Pupils become dilated
- Rise of body temperature and blood pressure
- Increase of activity, irritability, and nervousness
- Large doses may lead to a "speed run" (increased agitation, fearfulness, hallucinations, and possible psychosis)

Note: The use of these drugs can cause a strong psychological dependence. Withdrawing from these drugs can cause the user to experience extreme fatigue and become very depressed (crash). Cocaine is still classified as a narcotic, acting as a stimulant. (The addiction to cocaine can be so consuming that all survival functions—the need for food, water, sex, and protection—become secondary to the drive for cocaine.)

APPENDIX 2E:
MARIJUANA/HASHISH/THC
(Cannabis Sativa)

Street Names

Pot, grass, joint, jays, sticks, Mary Jane, reefer, roach (*hashish*—hash, Panama red, Acapulco gold—contains a stronger concentration of THC)

Medical Use

None

Route of Administration

Swallowed (sprinkled on food), smoked (using rolling paper or pipes)

Effects

- Sense of euphoria and a relaxation of inhibitions
- In the early stages of intoxication, there may be loud talking and inappropriate laughter
- Distortion of the senses and of perception
- Increase in appetite
- In the later stages, the user may be sleepy or stuporous
- Whites of the eyes are reddened
- An odor similar to burnt rope may cling to the clothes and breath

Note: It can take about 30 days for a single dose to be completely eliminated from the body. The drug available today is more potent than that which was available several years ago. Marijuana cigarette smoke has more cancer-causing substances than tobacco cigarette smoke. Long-term use can cause damage to the lungs, brain, and reproductive organs. Marijuana is often kept in small plastic bags. Stems and seeds may also be visible. Butts of the cigarettes (roaches) are saved for later use.

Drugs

Dilaudid, Talwin, Percodan, Darvon, morphine, methadone, codeine

Medical Use

a. Relief from pain
b. Codeine—cough suppressant; relief from pain
c. Paregoric—stop diarrhea; relief from tooth pain

Route of Administration

Ingestion, inhalation, injection

Effects

- Euphoria → drowsiness → becoming stuporous
- Pupils become constricted
- Nodding

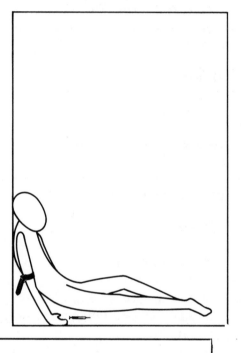

Illegal Drug

Heroin

Street Names of Heroin

Smack, stuff, scag, horse, dope

Medical Use

None

Note: Narcotics are highly addictive. There is danger of infection from using unsterilized equipment. The disease AIDS may be contracted by the use of contaminated needles and syringes. Needle marks or scars may be seen, usually on the arms. Syringes, bent spoons, bottle caps, cotton, eye droppers, or needles may be found.

APPENDIX 2G:
INHALANTS

Substances

Glue (especially airplane glue), nail polish remover, aerosol sprays, spot remover, lacquer, cleaning fluid, liquid correction fluid for typewriters

Street Names

Popper, bolt, locker room, rush, ames

Medical Use

None

Route of Administration

Inhalation

Effects

- May appear uncoordinated, dizzy, and confused
- May appear drunk or in a dreamlike state
- An odor of the substance can be detected on the breath and clothing
- Frequent nausea and vomiting
- Impaired judgment
- May have blue lips due to lack of oxygen
- Long-term use can cause damage to the brain, kidney, and liver

---

Note: Plastic bags may be used to intensify the results. If the user becomes unconscious, death can result due to suffocation. Paper bags or rags may be found in the area. Death can result from displacing oxygen in the lungs or by depressing the central nervous system causing respiratory arrest.

INHALANTS ARE LEGAL SUBSTANCES THAT ARE READILY AVAILABLE AND INEXPENSIVE. THEREFORE, THEY ARE USUALLY ABUSED BY CHILDREN!

APPENDIX 2H:
HALLUCINOGENS

Hallucinogens are drugs that precipitate imaginary visions, also known as hallucinations.

Drugs

LSD, PCP, mescaline, peyote

Street Names

Acid, angel dust, supergrass, killer weed, scramblers, blotter, buttons, cubes, mesc

Medical Use

None

Route of Administration

Ingestion. PCP may be inhaled or sprinkled on parsley or marijuana and smoked like a joint (marijuana cigarette).

Effects

- Senses of sight, hearing, as well as body image and time are distorted
- Perception, mood, and behavior are affected in a manner depending upon the emotional condition of the user and the environmental conditions
- Users may sit quietly in a dreamlike state
- There may be a feeling of depersonalization of body image and feelings of severe anxiety

---

Note: *LSD is a colorless, odorless, and tasteless drug. "Flashbacks" (re-experiencing the hallucinations) can occur without using the drug, over a long period of time. Experiences can vary each time the drug is taken. PCP has produced dangerous symptoms. Its use may precipitate violent, bizarre, and unpredictable behavior.*

APPENDIX 3:
SELF-HELP GROUPS

Here is information on various self-help groups:

Parents of Adolescents

TOUGH LOVE: Parent support groups for dealing with teenagers' unacceptable behavior. Help in starting groups, self-help manual, parent support network. Newsletter. TOUGH LOVE information line: (215) 348-7090, 9-5 P.M. (Eastern time). Write: TOUGH LOVE, Box 1069, Doylestown, PA 18901.

Alcoholism

ALCOHOLICS ANONYMOUS: Fellowship sharing experiences, strengths, and hopes with each other so they may solve common problems and help each other recover from alcoholism. Bimonthly newsletter "Loners Internationalist" includes networking by mail. Write: Box 459, Grand Central Station, New York, NY 10163. Call: (212) 686-1100.

ALATEEN: For younger family members who live in an alcoholic family situation to learn effective ways to cope with problems. Helps members achieve detachment from alcoholic family member. Newsletter, pen pal, "Loner's Service." Chapter development kit. Write: Al-Anon Family Group Headquarters, P.O. Box 182, Madison Square Station, New York, NY 10159. Call: (212) 683-1771.

AL-ANON FAMILY GROUP: Provides help for family members and friends of problem drinkers by offering comfort, hope, and friendship through shared experiences. "Lone Member Letterbox" newsletter. "Al-Anon Speaks Out" newsletter for professionals. Guidelines for developing new groups. Write: P.O. Box 182, Madison Square Station, New York, NY 10159-0182. Call: (212) 683-1771.

NATIONAL ASSOCIATION FOR CHILDREN OF ALCOHOLICS: Support and information for children of alcoholics of all ages and those in a position to help them. Write: NACOA, P.O. Box 421691, San Francisco, CA 94142.

Drug Abuse

NARCOTICS ANONYMOUS: Fellowship of recovering addicts meeting to "stay clean of all drugs." National newsletter. Write: 16155 Wyandotte Street, Van Nuys, CA 91406.

FAMILIES ANONYMOUS: For relatives and friends concerned about the use of drugs and alcohol or related behavioral problems. Referrals to local groups. Guidelines for developing groups. Newsletter "12-Step Rag." Write: P.O. Box 528, Van Nuys, CA 91408. Call: (818) 989-7841.

NAR-ANON FAMILY GROUPS: Fellowship of relatives and friends of drug abusers. Follows the 12-step program adapted from Alcoholics Anonymous and Al-Anon. Helps members learn to achieve peace of mind and gain hope for the future. Write: Nar-Anon Family Group Headquarters, P.O. Box 2562, Palos Verdes, CA 92704. Call: (213) 547–5800.

PILL-ANON: Self-help for friends and relatives of people dependent on mood-altering chemicals. Based on the 12-step recovery program of Alcoholics Anonymous. Newsletter. Chapter development guidelines. Write: P.O. Box 120, Gracie Square Station, New York, NY 10028. Call: (718) 361–2169.

DRUGS ANONYMOUS: Fellowship of men and women sharing experiences, strengths, and hopes, that they may recover from chemical dependency. Write: P.O. Box 473, Ansonia Station, New York, NY 10023. Call: (212) 874–0700.

PILL ADDICTS ANONYMOUS: Fellowship for all who seek freedom from addiction to mood-changing pills and drugs. Sharing experiences, strengths, and hopes, to stay sober and help others achieve sobriety. Pen pal program. Group development guidelines. Write: General Service Board of Pill Addicts Anonymous, P.O. Box 278, Reading, PA 19603. Call: (215) 372–1128.

NATIONAL FEDERATION OF PARENTS FOR DRUG-FREE YOUTH: Information, networking, newsletter, and guidelines for parents forming groups to address drug abuse problems among adolescents. Write: 1820 Franwall Avenue, Suite 16, Silver Spring, MD 20902. Call: (301) 649–7100 or (800) 554–KIDS.

Note: Special thanks to the New Jersey Self-Help Clearinghouse, St. Clare's Hospital in Denville, for their help in the preparation of Appendix 3.

APPENDIX 4:
STATE GOVERNMENT AGENCIES
FOR DRUG/ALCOHOL INFORMATION

ALABAMA

Division of Alcohol and Drug Abuse
502 Washington Avenue
Montgomery, Alabama 36130
(205) 834–4350, x332

ALASKA

Department of Health and Social Services
Office of Alcoholism and Drug Abuse
Pouch H/05F, 231 South Franklin
Juneau, Alaska 99611
(907) 586–6201

ARIZONA

Arizona Department of Health Services
Bureau of Community Services
Alcohol Abuse and Alcoholism Section
2500 East Van Buren Street
Phoenix, Arizona 85006
(602) 255–1420

ARKANSAS

Office on Alcohol and Drug Abuse
  Prevention
1515 West 7th Street, Suite 300
Little Rock, Arkansas 72202
(501) 371–2604

CALIFORNIA

Department of Alcohol and Drug Programs
111 Capitol Mall Suite 450
Sacramento, California 95814
(916) 445–1940

COLORADO

Department of Health
Alcohol and Drug Abuse Division
4210 East 11th Avenue
Denver, Colorado 80220
(303) 320–6137

CONNECTICUT

Connecticut Alcohol and Drug Abuse
  Commission
999 Asylum Avenue
Hartford, Connecticut 06105
(203) 566–4145

DELAWARE

Division of Mental Health
Bureau of Alcoholism and Drug Abuse
1901 North DuPont Highway
New Castle, Delaware 19720
(302) 421–6101

WASHINGTON, D.C.

Office of Health Planning and Development
1875 Connecticut Avenue, N.W.
Suite 836A
Washington, D.C. 20009
(202) 673–6723

FLORIDA

Mental Health Program Office
Alcoholism Rehabilitation Program
1323 Winewood Boulevard
Tallahassee, Florida 32301
(904) 487–2820 and 2830

GEORGIA

Division of Mental Health and Mental
  Retardation
Alcoholism and Drug Abuse Services Station
47 Trinity Avenue, S.W.
Atlanta, Georgia 30345
(404) 894–4785

237

GUAM

Department of Mental Health and Substance
  Abuse
P.O. Box 8896
Tamuning, Guam 96911
(671) 646–9261/2/3

HAWAII

Department of Health
Alcohol and Drug Abuse Branch
P.O. Box 3378
Honolulu, Hawaii 96801
(806) 548–4280

IDAHO

Department of Health and Welfare
Substance Abuse Section
450 West State, 4th Floor
Boise, Idaho 83720
(208) 334–4368

ILLINOIS

Department of Alcoholism and Substance
  Abuse
300 N. State Street
Suite 1500
Chicago, Illinois 60610
(312) 822–9860

INDIANA

Division of Addiction Services
5 Indiana Square
Indianapolis, Indiana 46204
(317) 232–7816

IOWA

Department of Substance Abuse
505 5th Avenue, Suite 202
Des Moines, Iowa 50319
(515) 281–3641

KANSAS

Alcohol and Drug Abuse Services
Department of Social and Rehabilitative
  Services
Biddle Building
2700 West 6th Street, 2nd Floor
Topeka, Kansas 66606
(913) 296–3925

KENTUCKY

Bureau for Health Services
275 East Main Street
Frankfort, Kentucky 40621
(502) 564–3970

LOUISIANA

Office of Alcohol and Substance Abuse
  Prevention and Rehabilitation
P.O. Box 4049
Baton Rouge, Louisiana 70821
(504) 342–2548

MAINE

Office of Alcoholism and Drug Abuse
  Prevention
State House Station II
Augusta, Maine 04333
(207) 289–2781

MARIANA

Mariana Islands
Division of Mental Health
Saipan, Mariana Islands 96950

MARYLAND

Alcoholism Control Administration
201 West Preston Street
Baltimore, Maryland 21201
(301) 383–4082

MASSACHUSETTS

Department of Public Health
Division of Alcoholism
150 Tremont Street
Boston, Massachusetts 02111
(617) 727–1960

MICHIGAN

Office of Substance Abuse Services
3500 North Logan Street
P.O. Box 30035
Lansing, Michigan 48909
(517) 373–8603

MINNESOTA

Chemical Dependency Program Division
Department of Human Services
Centennial Office Building, 4th Floor
658 Cedar Street
St. Paul, Minnesota 55155
(612) 296–3991

MISSISSIPPI

Division of Alcohol and Drug Abuse
1102 Robert E. Lee Office Building
Jackson, Mississippi 39201
(601) 359–1297

MISSOURI

Division of Alcohol and Drug Abuse
P.O. Box 687
Jefferson City, Missouri 65101
(314) 751–4942

MONTANA

Alcohol and Drug Abuse Division
1539 11th Avenue
Helena, Montana 59601
(406) 449–2827

NEBRASKA

Division on Alcoholism
Box 94728
Lincoln, Nebraska 68509
(402) 471–2851, x415

NEVADA

Bureau of Alcohol and Drug Abuse
5th Floor Kinkead Building
505 East King Street
Carson City, Nevada 89710
(702) 885–4790

NEW HAMPSHIRE

Office of Alcohol and Drug Abuse
  Prevention
Health and Welfare Building, Hazen Drive
Concord, New Hampshire 03301
(603) 271–4627 and 4630

NEW JERSEY

Division of Alcoholism
State Department of Health
129 East Hanover Street
Trenton, New Jersey 08608
(609) 292–8949

NEW MEXICO

Alcoholism Bureau
BHSD, Health and Environment Department
P.O. Box 968
Santa Fe, New Mexico 87504
(505) 984–0020, x493

NEW YORK

Division of Alcoholism and Alcohol Abuse
194 Washington Avenue
Albany, New York 12210
(518) 474–5417

NORTH CAROLINA

Division of Mental Health, Mental
  Retardation and Substance Abuse
Alcohol and Drug Abuse Services
Albemarle Building, Room 1100
325 North Salisbury Street
Raleigh, North Carolina 27611
(919) 733–4670

NORTH DAKOTA

Department of Health
State Capitol
Bismarck, North Dakota 58501
(701) 224–2370

OHIO

Bureau of Alcohol Abuse and Alcoholism
  Recovery
170 North High Street, P.O. Box 118
Columbus, Ohio 43216
(614) 466–3445

OKLAHOMA

Division of Alcoholism
P.O. Box 53277, Capitol Station
Oklahoma City, Oklahoma 73152
(405) 521–2811

OREGON

Mental Health Division
Programs for Alcohol and Drug Problems
2575 Bittern, N.E.
Salem, Oregon 97310
(503) 378–2163

PENNSYLVANIA

Department of Health
Office of Drug and Alcohol Programs
Room 809, Health and Welfare Building
Harrisburg, Pennsylvania 17108
(717) 787–9857

PUERTO RICO

Department of Addiction Services
Box B-Y
Rio Piedras Station
Rio Piedras, Puerto Rico 00928
(809) 763–5014

RHODE ISLAND

Division of Substance Abuse
General Hospital, Building 303
R.I. Medical Center
Cranston, Rhode Island 02920
(401) 464–2091

AMERICAN SAMOA

Mental Health Clinic
Pago, Pago, American Samoa 96779

SOUTH CAROLINA

South Carolina Commission on Alcohol
  and Drug Abuse
3700 Forest Drive, Suite 300
Columbia, South Carolina 29204
(803) 758–2521

SOUTH DAKOTA

Division of Alcohol and Drug Abuse
Joe Foss Building
523 E. Capital
Pierre, South Dakota 57501-3182
(605) 773–3146

TENNESSEE

Division of Alcohol and Drug Abuse
  Services
James K. Polk State Office Building
4th Floor
505 Deaderick Street
Nashville, Tennessee 37219
(615) 741–1921

TEXAS

Texas Commission on Alcoholism
1705 Guadalupe Street
Austin, Texas 78701
(512) 475–2577

UTAH

Division of Alcoholism and Drugs
P.O. Box 2500, Room 340
Salt Lake City, Utah 84110
(801) 533–6532

VERMONT

Office of Alcohol and Drug Abuse Programs
Waterbury Complex
103 South Main Street
Waterbury, Vermont 05676
(802) 241–2170

VIRGINIA

Office of Substance Abuse Services
Department of Mental Health and Mental
   Retardation
P.O. Box 1797
Richmond, Virginia 23214
(804) 786–1524

VIRGIN ISLANDS

Division of Mental Health
Alcoholism and Drug Dependency
P.O. Box 520
Christiansted, St. Croix
U.S. Virgin Islands 00820
(809) 774–4888

WASHINGTON

Bureau of Alcohol and Substance Abuse
Mailstop OB-44W
Olympia, Washington 96504
(206) 753–5866

WEST VIRGINIA

Division on Alcoholism and Drug Abuse
State Capitol
Charleston, West Virginia 25305
(304) 348–2276

WISCONSIN

Office of Alcohol and Other Drug Abuse
1 West Wilson Street, Room 441
P.O. Box 7851
Madison, Wisconsin 53702
(608) 266–2717

WYOMING

Division of Community Programs
Hathaway Building
Cheyenne, Wyoming 82002
(307) 777–7115

---

*Note: Educational material, much of it free, is available from the National
Clearinghouse for Alcohol Information, Box 2345, Rockville,
Maryland 20852. Telephone Number (301) 468–2600*

Here are the answer keys to six of the activity sheets:

4–12A   AN ALCOHOL WORD SEARCH

```
T  M  C  O  O  K  L  S  P  B
L  R  E  L  I  G  I  O  U  S
P  I  L  A  C  M  Z  W  B  E
O  D  E  P  L  A  Y  G  R  R
S  E  B  R  O  T  S  E  J  V
O  U  R  A  P  A  I  N  T  I
B  O  A  C  M  T  E  M  Z  C
E  M  T  S  O  I  L  Q  E  E
F  T  E  N  G  J  M  D  L  S
L  R  N  E  B  A  L  L  H  K
```

5–1A   LABEL CANS, NOT PEOPLE

1. LAZY
2. SICK
3. BAD
4. DUMB
5. CRAZY
6. STUPID
7. NERD
8. CREEP
9. SLOW
10. SISSY

6–7C   GOING UP IN SMOKE

7–8C   PACK OF CIGARETTES

```
Y  M  T  A  R  S  B  C  T  L  O  R  W
X  T  O  X  Y  G  E  N  E  U  X  E  I
B  S  B  R  E  A  T  H  E  N  Y  S  T
W  R  A  F  H  Q  R  S  T  G  K  T  H
V  T  C  O  A  L  T  A  H  V  E  A  D
C  P  C  T  P  O  L  L  U  T  E  S  R
U  Q  O  U  V  W  Z  X  K  L  M  A
T  B  T  R  E  A  T  S  O  W  I  T  W
D  A  A  D  A  N  G  E  R  S  D  R  A
S  M  R  E  S  T  A  U  R  A  N  T  L
```

7–12B   BUMPER STICKERS

1. ALCOHOL IS A DRUG
2. I CAN LEARN TO FACE MY PROBLEMS
3. ALCOHOLISM IS A DISEASE
4. I CAN MAKE CHOICES
5. ONLY SICK PEOPLE NEED DRUGS

7–12C   ALL ABOUT ALCOHOL

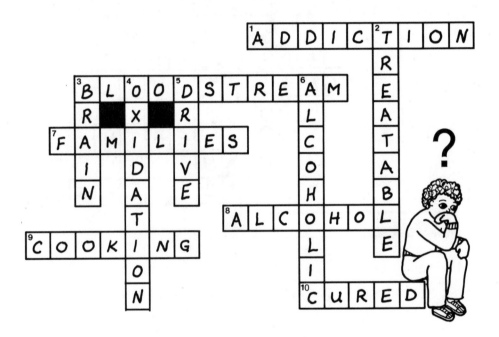